Birmingham Repertory Theatre Company and Kali presents

MUSTAFA

by Naylah Ahmed

First performed at Soho Theatre on 7 March 2012

Mustafa

by Naylah Ahmed

Mustafa	**Munir Khairdin**
Shabir	**Gary Pillai**
Dan	**Ryan Early**
Len	**Paul McCleary**

Director	**Janet Steel**
Designer	**Colin Falconer**
Lighting Designer	**Tim Mitchell**
Music	**Arun Ghosh**
Dramaturg	**Caroline Jester**
Casting Director	**Alison Solomon**
Stage Illusionist	**Richard Pinner**
Company Stage Manager	**Jessica Thanki**
Assistant Stage Manager	**Phillip Richardson**

Cast

Munir Khairdin *Mustafa*
Munir trained at Arts Educational.

Theatre credits include: *The Comedy of Errors* (Manchester Royal Exchange); *As You Like It* (Curve Leicester); *Gone Too Far, The Arsonists* (Royal Court, London); *Foxes* (West Yorkshire Playhouse); *The Hot Zone, Sleeping Around* (Lyric Hammersmith); *Calcutta Kosher, Rashomon* (Library Theatre, Manchester): *Behzti* (Birmingham Repertory Theatre); *Romeo and Juliet* (Hazlitt Theatre); *Bombay Dreams* (Apollo Theatre); *The Butcher's Skin* (Yellow Earth tour); *Ramayana Odyssey* (Tara Arts tour); Kafka's *The Trial, The Merchant of Venice* (Cherub Company tour); *Romeo and Juliet* (Haymarket).

Television and film credits include: *Silk, Sherlock* (BBC); *Hustle, Spooks* (Kudos); *The Shadow Line* (Company Pictures); *The Passion* (HBO/BBC); *Britz* (Mentorn Films); *Operation Stormhouse* (Company Scanner); *Bad Moon Rising* (Mad Mile Productions); *Extraordinary Rendition* (Ultra Films Ltd).

Radio credits include: *An Enemy of the People, Pandemic.*

Gary Pillai *Shabir*
Theatre credits include: *Tagore's Women, Gandhi and Coconuts* (Kali Theatre Company); *Wuthering Heights* (Tamasha/Lyric Hammersmith); *Much Ado About Nothing* (National Theatre); Krishna in *Mahabharata* (Sadler's Wells); *Cancer Tales* (New Wolsey, Ipswich); *A Passage to India* (Shared Experience/London/New York); *The Good Woman of Setzuan, Macbeth, An Ideal Husband, Bollywood Jane, The Witches, Death of a Salesman, The White Devil, Richard III* (Leicester Haymarket); *Unsuitable Girls* (Pilot Theatre/Contact Theatre, Manchester); *Oedipus, Don Juan* (BAC); *Staying On* (Yvonne Arnaud/Shaftesbury Theatre); *Suzuki* (Royal Court, London); *The Moonstone* (Manchester Royal Exchange); *The Tempest, Troilus and Cressida* (Tara Arts).

Television credits include: *Coronation Street, Dirk Gently, Emmerdale, Survivors, Torchwood, The Passion, Dalziel & Pascoe, Green Eyed Monster, Mysterious Creatures, The Bill, Adventure Inç, Footballers' Wives, Family Affairs, Men Only, Choices.*

Film credits include: *Tooting Broadway, Franklyn, Far North, Green Green Lanes, A Short Film About Swearing, The Waiting Room, How I Became Indian.*

Radio credits include: *Sparkhill Sound, The Archers, Funny Boy/Book at Bedtime, Patricia's Progress.*

Ryan Early *Dan*
Ryan trained at Drama Centre London.

Theatre credits include: *Amy's View*, *The Secret Garden* (Nottingham Playhouse); *Alice in Wonderland*, *Starseeker* (Royal & Derngate, Northampton); *The Interview* (Arcola Theatre, London); *The Hounding of David Oluwale* (West Yorkshire Playhouse/ national tour); *All Quiet on the Western Front* (Nottingham Playhouse/national tour); *War and Peace*, *The Eleventh Capital*, *Teeth 'N' Smiles* (Royal Court, London); *Beau Brummell* (Theatre 59E59, New York); *Miss Yesterday* (Stephen Joseph Theatre); *The Knight of the Burning Pestle* (Young Vic); *About Face* (Almeida Studio); *Oliver Twist* (Lyric Hammersmith/national tour); *The Country Wife* (Watford Palace Theatre); *A Midsummer Night's Dream*, *The Golden Ass* (Shakespeare's Globe); *The Servant* (Lyric Hammersmith); *Spring and Portwine* (West Yorkshire Playhouse); *One Life and Counting* (Bush Theatre, London).

Television credits include: *Coronation Street*, *Doctors*, *Margot and Mez*, *Casualty*, *Soup Kitchen*, *The Bill*, *Love Soup*, *Heartbeat*, *The Detective*.

Film credits include: *Red Tails*, *An Acre of Moon*, *Besame Mucho*.

Paul McCleary *Len*
Paul trained at Bristol Old Vic Theatre School.

Theatre credits include: *The Taming of the Shrew*, *The Happy End*, *Real Dreams*, *The Danton Affair*, *The Merchant of Venice*, *Much Ado About Nothing*, *The Tempest* (Royal Shakespeare Company); *Juno and the Paycock*, *Hove*, *Oedipus*, *Greenland* (National Theatre). Recent theatre credits include: Ubu in *The Trial of Ubu* (Hampstead Theatre, London); Leo (Head Chef) in *The Kitchen* (National Theatre); *'Tis Pity She's a Whore*, *They Sing Faster in the City* (Liverpool Everyman); *The Fairy Queen* (Glyndebourne/Paris/New York); *King of the Gypsies* (Edinburgh Festival). Paul has worked at most of the UK's regional theatres and in Tokyo, Los Angeles, New York, Portugal, Hungary, France, Spain, Vietnam, Malaysia, Saudi Arabia, Kuwait and Hong Kong.

Television credits include: *Boon*, *Billy*, *Max and Paddy's Road to Nowhere*, *Peak Practice*, *The Extraordinary Equiano*, *Doctors*.

Film credits include: *Prostitute*, *Britannia Hospital*, *Calendar Girls*.

Radio credits include: *The Voyage Out*, *The Crowded Street*, *Stone*.

Creative Team

Naylah Ahmed Writer
Birmingham writer Naylah Ahmed has been writing since the late 1990s for stage, radio and television. She won the Bruntwood Prize for Playwriting with *Butcher Boys* in 2008, and was one of the writers of *These Four Streets*, which premiered at Birmingham Repertory Theatre in 2009.

Janet Steel Director
Artistic Director of Kali Theatre since 2003.

After many years as an actress, Janet's directing career began in 1988 at Loose Change Theatre with her first full-length piece, *White Biting Dog*. Directing credits include: *Behzti* (Birmingham Repertory Theatre); *April in Paris*, *Bretevski Street*, *A Hard Rain*, *Top Girls* (Northampton Royal); *Millennium Mysteries*, *Big School* (Belgrade Coventry); *Antigone*, *The Mother*, *Orpheus Descending*, *An Ideal Husband*, *Romeo and Juliet*, *The Knockey*, *Serious Money* (Rose Bruford College).

For Kali Theatre credits include: *Calcutta Kosher*, *Chaos*, *Paper Thin*, *Deadeye*, *Zameen*, *Another Paradise*, *Behna*, *Gandhi and Coconuts*, *Purnjanam/Born Again*.

Colin Falconer Designer
Colin studied Interior and Environmental Design at Duncan of Jordanstone College, University of Dundee and Theatre Design at Nottingham Trent University.

He has designed productions of *The Importance of Being Earnest*, *Travesties* (Birmingham Repertory Theatre); *The Constant Wife*, *The Picture*, *Private Lives*, *The Winslow Boy*, *Restoration*, *Northanger Abbey* (Salisbury Playhouse); *The Rime of the Ancient Mariner* (Southbank Centre); *Barabas* (Hall for Cornwall); *The Graft* (Theatre Royal Stratford East); *Blithe Spirit* (Watford Palace Theatre); *Plunder* (Watermill Theatre/Greenwich Theatre); *Outlying Islands* (Theatre Royal Bath); *The House of Bernarda Alba*, *Siwan*, *Cariad*, *Mr Bustl*, *Endgame*, *Dominos* (Theatr Genedlaethol Cymru); *Anansi Trades Places* (Talawa Theatre Company); *Maes Terfyn* (Sherman Cymru); *Madam T* (Meridien Theatre Company, Cork); *Romeo and Juliet*, *Three Sisters* (Chichester Festival Theatre); *The Merchant of Venice* (Royal Shakespeare Company); *The Misanthrope*, *The Secret Rapture*, *Hysteria* (Minerva Theatre, Chichester); *The Blue Room* (Theatre Royal Haymarket); *Acis and Galatea*, *Dido and Aeneas*, *Hansel und Gretel* (RSAMD, Glasgow); *Aladdin* (Costumes, Scottish Ballet); *Twelfth Night* (Liverpool Playhouse).

www.colinfalconer.co.uk

Tim Mitchell Lighting Designer

Theatre includes: *Singin' in the Rain* (West End/Chichester Festival Theatre); *Crazy For You* (West End/Regent's Park); *Earthquakes in London* (Headlong); *Smash* (Menier Chocolate Factory); *Racing Demon, An Enemy of the People* (Sheffield Crucible); *Tell Me on a Sunday* (tour); *Master Class* (Theatre Royal Bath); *Filumena, The Knot of the Heart, Becky Shaw* (Almeida Theatre); *The Syndicate, Goodnight Mr Tom, The Critic/Real Inspector Hound, Bingo* (also Young Vic), *The Master Builder, Oklahoma* (Chichester Festival Theatre, for whom he is an associate); *The Cherry Orchard, Arthur & George* (Birmingham Repertory Theatre); *Dirty Dancing* (UK tour/ West End/ Toronto/ Hamburg/Utrecht/USA tour/ Berlin); *The History Boys* (West Yorkshire Playhouse/tour); *Alphabetical Order* (also tour), *Darker Shores, Amongst Friends* (Hampstead Theatre); *A Month in the Country* (Salisbury Playhouse); *Cinderella* (Old Vic); *Sleeping Beauty* (New York/Barbican/Young Vic); *Henry IV Parts I and II* (Washington Shakespeare); *The Play What I Wrote* (Broadway /West End); *Merrily We Roll Along* (Donmar Warehouse); *Hamlet* (Japan/Sadler's Wells) and *Yes, Prime Minister, Imagine This, Bad Girls the Musical, Otherwise Engaged, As You Like It, Romeo and Juliet, Of Mice and Men* (West End). Working extensively with the RSC, his recent credits include: *Written on the Heart, The City Madam, Cardenio, Morte D'Arthur, Twelfth Night* and *Hamlet*.

Opera and dance includes: *A Streetcar Named Desire* (Scottish Ballet); *Ariadne auf Naxos* (WNO/Boston); *La Bohème, Die Fledermaus* (WNO); *Die Frau ohne Schatten, Elektra* (Opera de Nice/Mariinsky, Russia); productions for NBT, BRB, ROH and Sadler's Wells.

Arun Ghosh Music

Arun Ghosh is a British Asian clarinettist, composer and music educator. He has released two critically acclaimed albums, *Northern Namaste* (2008) and *Primal Odyssey* (2011) on camoci records. Other significant works are *A South Asian Suite*, and a live score to Lotte Reiniger's *The Adventures of Prince Achmed*.

Recent theatre work includes: *Tagore's Women* (with Kali Theatre), *The Snow Queen* (Unicorn Theatre). Other theatre work includes: *Volpone, The Tempest, Antigone* (Manchester Royal Exchange); *Indian Ink* (Salisbury Playhouse); *And did those feet...* (Bolton Octagon); *Storm* by Lemn Sissay (Contact, Manchester).

Radio work includes: *The Healing Pool* (Radio 4); *Bora Bistrah* (Radio 3).

Dance composition includes: *Song of the City* (Akademi); *Fading Contact, The Art of Travel* (Kadam); *Sacred Move, The Saptarishi* (Chaturangan).

He is currently working on a new commission to be performed at the BT River of Music festival as part of the London 2012 Cultural Olympiad, and a rescoring of *Prince Achmed* to be performed at the Boulevard Festival, Morocco.

Arun performs and tours nationally and internationally with his IndoJazz ensembles and will be releasing *A South Asian Suite* this autumn.

Caroline Jester Dramaturg
Caroline is Dramaturg at Birmingham Repertory Theatre and has taught on the MPhil in Playwriting at Birmingham University and various undergraduate programmes. She is the co-author of *Playwriting Across the Curriculum*, published by Routledge, and has worked as a freelance dramaturg, director and workshop leader.

Alison Solomon Casting Director
As Casting Director for Birmingham Repertory Theatre credits include: *Gravity*, community cast for *The Wiz*, *Notes to Future Self*, *Respect*, *Behna* (*Sisters*), *Grass Routes Festival*, *East is East* (with Sooki McShane as lead Casting Director), *These Four Streets*, British cast for *Looking For Yoghurt* (Birmingham Repertory Theatre, Joyful Theatre and Kijimuna Festa in association with Hanyong Theatre), *Rosetta Life*, *Toy Theatres*, *The Speckled Monster* (Birmingham Repertory Theatre in Association with University of Birmingham), *At the Gates of Gaza* (Big Creative Ideas in Association with Birmingham Repertory Theatre), *360 Degrees* (*Generation*), Transmissions Festival, The Big 10.

Norman Beaton Fellowship 2012, 2011, 2010 & 2008 – BBC Radio Drama (Birmingham) and Birmingham Repertory Theatre.

As Children's Casting Director for Birmingham Repertory Theatre credits include: *A Christmas Carol*, *The Grapes of Wrath*, *Orphans*, *Once on this Island*, *An Inspector Calls*, *Hapgood*, *Peter Pan*, *Wizard of Oz*, *Galileo*.

Recent workshops/readings include: *Gravity*, *Shell Shock*, *Bookface*, *Mustafa*, *Transmissions*, *Without Parade*, *Our House*, *Pwnage*, *Broken Stones*, *Notes to Future Self*, *Grass Routes Workshops*, *Coming Out From the Cold*, *Fairytale Toy Theatres*, *Dealing With Dreams*, *Cling to Me Like Ivy*, *Respect*, *Dirty Fingernails*, *Engaged*, *After Magritte*, *In Extremis*, *Handbag*.

Jessica Thanki Company Stage Manager
Jessica has a BA in Theatre Production. Since graduating she has stage-managed the following shows: *The Maid* (Odd Man Out Productions at Rich Mix); *Double Dutch Espresso* (Theatre Waah at Tristan Bates); *Measure for Measure* (BADA at Ovalhouse); *Maybe Father* (Talawa at The Young Vic); *Behna 2010*, *Behna 2011* (Kali with Birmingham Repertory Theatre and Black Country Touring); *It Hasn't Happened Yet* (Liz Carr tour); *SQUID* (school tour for Theatre Royal Stratford East); *Brixton Rocks* (Tara Arts). Company stage-managed *Black-i* (Kali Theatre at Ovalhouse); *Gandhi and Coconuts* (Kali Theatre at Arcola Theatre/tour). Shortlisted for Stage Manager of the Year 2011.

Phillip Richardson Assistant Stage Manager
Stage Management credits include: *Same Same* (Ovalhouse); *66 Books* (Bush Theatre, London); *Tonight Sandy Grierson will Lecture, Dance, Box* (Edinburgh Festival); *Theatre Brothel* (UK tour); *Landscape* and *Monologue* (Bath Ustinov Studio); *Stuck in the Throat* (Hen and Chickens Theatre/Exeter Fringe Festival); *So On and So Forth* (Accidental Festival/Edinburgh Festival); *The York Realist* (Riverside Studios); *State Fair, Generous* (Finborough Theatre); *Olive Juice* (Lion and Unicorn Theatre); *The Collector* (Etcetera Theatre); *Oleanna* (Leeds Carriageworks).

With thanks to Jason Burg

THEATRE COMPANY

Kali has been presenting groundbreaking new theatre writing by women with a South Asian background for over twenty years. We seek out and nurture strong individual writers who challenge our perceptions through original and thought-provoking theatre. We actively encourage our writers to reinvent and reshape the theatrical agenda. **Kali** presents the distinct perspective and experience of South Asian women, engaging people from all backgrounds in work that reflects and comments on our lives today.

Find our more or join our mailing list via
www.kalitheatre.co.uk

For Kali Theatre
Artistic Director   Janet Steel
General Manager   Christopher Corner
Audience Development Manager   Binita Walia
Marketing & Press   Yasmeen Khan

Birmingham Repertory Theatre Company

Communications & PR Manager
Clare Jepson-Homer

Marketing & Communications Officer
Eleanor Miles

Digital Officer
Clare Lovell

Development Manager
Anya Simpson

Development Officer
Ros Adams

Development Office
Kayleigh Cottam (Maternity cover)

REP 100 Archive Researcher
Sara Crathorne

Theatre Manager
Nigel Cairns

Sales Manager
Gerard Swift

Sales Team Supervisor
Rebecca Thorndyke

Sales Development Supervisor
Rachel Foster

Sales Team
Anne Bower
Kayleigh Cottam
Sebastian Maynard-Francis
Eileen Minnock

Stage Door Reception
Tracey Dolby
Robert Flynn

Cleaning by
We Clean Limited

Head of Production
Tomas Wright

Production Manager
Milorad Zakula

Production Assistant
Hayley Seddon

Head of Stage
Adrian Bradley

Head of Lighting
Andrew Fidgeon

Lighting Design Technician
Simon Bond

Head of Sound
Dan Hoole

Deputy Head of Sound
Clive Meldrum

Company Manager
Ruth Morgan

Workshop Supervisor
Margaret Rees

Construction Coordinator
Oliver Shapley

Deputy Workshop Supervisor
Simon Fox

Head Scenic Artist
Christopher Tait

Head of Wardrobe
Sue Nightingale

Wardrobe
Liz Vass

Head of Wigs and Make-up
Andrew Whiteoak

With thanks to the following volunteers
Student REPresentatives

REP Archivist
Horace Gillis

THE REP

A CHANGE OF SCENERY

Birmingham Repertory Theatre

Birmingham Repertory Theatre is one of Britain's leading producing theatre companies. Founded nearly 100 years ago by Sir Barry Jackson, the company will celebrate its centenary in 2013.

As a pioneer of new plays, the commissioning and production of new work lies at the core of The REP's programme and over the last five years the company has produced more than 130 new plays.

The REP's productions regularly transfer to London and tour nationally and internationally. Recent tours have included: *The Snowman* which made its international debut in Korea in 2009 and performed in Birmingham, Salford and Finland in 2011, a new staging of Philip Pullman's *His Dark Materials*, the world premiere of Dennis Kelly's *Orphans*, Simon Stephens' *Pornography*, Lucy Caldwell's *Notes to Future Self*, Samantha Ellis's *Cling To Me Like Ivy*, *Looking For Yoghurt* – a new play for young children which played at theatres in the UK, Japan and Korea – and *These Four Streets* – a multi-authored play about the 2005 Lozells disturbances.

Developing new and particularly younger audiences is also at the heart of The REP's work. The theatre's Learning and Participation department engages with over 10,000 young people each year through various initiatives including The Young REP, REP's Children, Grass Routes writing programme for 18–30 year olds and the Transmissions Playwriting programme in schools.

The REP is currently undergoing re-development as part of the new Library of Birmingham, which is due to open in 2013. This new partnership will see the two cultural venues sharing public spaces and a new purpose-built 300-seat auditorium. This marks a significant period in the history of The REP and it brings an exciting time artistically as audiences are currently able to enjoy and experience an imaginative programme of REP productions in other theatres and non-theatrical spaces across Birmingham.

The company has also recently announced the appointment of Roxana Silbert as artistic director. Roxana will join The REP for the company's centenary celebrations and return to its newly-developed building in 2013.

Artistic Director (Designate) Roxana Silbert
Executive Director Stuart Rogers

Box Office: 0121 236 4455
Administration: 0121 245 2000
birmingham-rep.co.uk

MUSTAFA

Naylah Ahmed

For my parents, Wazir and Perveen Ahmed

With special thanks to Caroline Jester, for not letting go…

Characters

MUSTAFA, *late thirties; a prisoner*
SHABIR, *early forties; a solicitor, Mustafa's brother*
DAN, *thirties; a prison officer*
LEN, *sixties; senior prison officer*

Mustafa is wearing a taveez on a black cord around his neck throughout the play.

Both Mustafa and Shabir came to England as children. They do not have Asian accents. Shabir is well spoken; he pronounces Urdu/Islamic words in an anglicised way. Mustafa's pronunciation will be correct in both Arabic and Urdu for someone with Pakistani heritage; he's not as posh as his brother.

Square brackets [ ] indicate speech that's intended but not said, or interrupted before the bracketed words.

An ellipsis (…) indicates an unspoken or unfinished thought.

The author requests that no real religious books/text/Qur'ān be used in production to avoid any unintended disrespect. With thanks.

This text went to press before the end of rehearsals and so may differ slightly from the play as performed.

Scene One

Day. A single-occupancy cell in an old, previously disused, wing of a UK prison. The cell is fronted with bars and looks onto a corridor. The cell door is open and the contents of the cell (bed, sheets, books, paper and some bits of chalk) are strewn all over the place. DAN, a prison officer, is looking for something – keeping one eye on the door to the corridor. LEN, a senior prison officer, enters. He looks disapprovingly at DAN, who keeps working.

LEN. What's going on here?

DAN (*jumps*). Eh?

LEN. What you doing?

DAN. Jesus, Len! Cell search – legit.

LEN. We've only just moved him in here. (*Enters cell.*) What did you think you'd find?

DAN. He doesn't eat anything – you noticed? I been watching him – close. Lads did a search last week – found zilch. There's a twenty in it if I find something, apparently!

LEN. I don't believe it...

DAN. Someone's gotta be smuggling some grub in for him... Just dunno who or where the hell he stashes it. Thought, now he's been moved, it might be easier to find... Anyway, gotta confiscate something, haven't we – keep him on his toes?

LEN. We?

DAN. Yeah – me and the lads.

LEN. You soft sap, the lads are out there having a coffee and another ginger biscuit probably – who do you think's gonna get in trouble if the guv finds out you been in here for no reason?

DAN isn't listening – he's crawled under the bed and we only see his legs as he searches around. LEN looks around the cell. He picks up a book that is strewn somewhere in the cell and places it on the shelf.

Show some respect, Dan.

DAN (*crawls out from under the bed*). What?

LEN. His books, they're religious, you know…

DAN. Yeah, course I do – didn't mess with his Qur'ān – it's over there.

The Qur'ān is sitting in the sink.

LEN. In the sink?

DAN. Yeah – I've been careful, don't worry. Wouldn't wanna risk him getting upset now, would I? He doesn't read 'em anyway – think he's got 'em all down by heart you know.

LEN. Yeah, he's a right clever so-and-so – unlike some I could mention. (*Pulling the book out and wiping it.*) Ah, what's the use?

LEN *picks up any other books he can see on the floor and places them on the shelf.*

DAN. I don't get it… I've looked everywhere – he ain't got anything in here.

LEN. Like what?

DAN. No KitKats, no crisps – not even a bleedin' mint!

LEN. He'll be done with his solicitor soon – so you better get it sorted in two [minutes]. Dan, are you listening, son, it is not 'legit' to go through his things over a bet!

DAN. You're not gonna grass me up, are ya?

LEN. Not if you put it all right by the time he gets back in here. Confiscating something doesn't mean you trash his cell.

DAN. Just a bet with the lads, that's all – freak's got everyone wondering what he's up to, 'specially after [today] –

LEN. They know what he's in for and they're using it to spook each other out. Think his solicitor's trying to get an appeal. Let's hope he's successful.

DAN. You are kidding, right? After what he done?

LEN. I'm not saying let him off – just… we're full up in here as it is.

DAN. Full up everywhere's what they'll say. Couldn't give us a hand?

LEN *folds his arms.* DAN *starts to clear up.*

LEN. This guy's more trouble than we bargained for.

DAN. D'you hear what happened lunchtime?

LEN. Yeah, I heard.

DAN. And?

LEN (*gives in and starts helping* DAN). And – two prisoners got into a ruck, happens every so often – it shouldn't be a surprise.

DAN. Yeah, but it wasn't any old ruck –

LEN. It was a fight, Dan.

DAN. Well, I was there – I was looking right at him –

LEN. Really? And what is your specific interest in this prisoner?

DAN. It's my job! Anyway, point is I was standing right there when Tony kicked off – that's the thing, this geezer looks all quiet and weedy but he smashed Tony right in the face with his –

LEN. I'm having a word with him about it tomorrow, all right?

DAN. Better you than me, man, talk about drawing the short straw, eh, Len – don't think there's many people wanna be in a room with him.

LEN. I'm his personal officer – that's the end of it.

DAN. Yeah, but –

LEN. Zip it.

DAN. I know, but –

LEN. We're supposed to be keeping it calm in here, okay? We start getting excited and we're all screwed. Focus. And if you can't do that then we should at least…

LEN *trails off as he looks down on the floor. There is a circle drawn on the floor in chalk.*

DAN (*overexcited*).What is it?

LEN. Don't know – just a circle – d'you see any chalk in here?

DAN (*looks around*). Yep!

LEN. Why'd he be drawing circles on the floor?

DAN. Maybe it's some magic witchcraft stuff?

LEN. Give over.

DAN. Shall we make him clean it off?

LEN. Why?

DAN. Cos… I dunno.

LEN. It's a bit of chalk, Dan. Did he do it in the other block?

DAN. What, when he was in with a cellmate? No chance, we'd have heard about it. Probably got excited now he's in isolation, can do what he likes.

LEN. Except eat KitKats, apparently.

LEN *gets up and dusts himself off.*

Closed this block off years ago – can't believe we're back.

DAN. Were you here when this bit was open?

LEN. Yeah, remember when they closed it off too.

DAN. Man, you're old.

LEN. Thank you. (*Looking around.*) Barely passed the safety, I bet.

DAN. Should make him feel right at home – magic Mustafa.

LEN. Oi! It's thanks to comments like that he's in here, on his lonesome. Keep getting excited and he'll be in here for longer than we can manage – means we've got to make the trek over to check on him.

DAN. 'S just one extra corridor, Len.

LEN. Yeah, might be to you, but some of us could do without the extra exercise. Can't get the staff as it is.

DAN. Thanks a lot!

LEN. Pleasure's all mine.

End of scene.

Fade.

Scene Two

Same day, continuous. A room for prisoner meetings with their legal representatives – known amongst the prison staff as 'the goldfish bowl', as it has a large glass window for officers outside to keep an eye. A table and two chairs sit in the middle of the room. SHABIR, a solicitor, is seated with a briefcase of files beside him. MUSTAFA, a prisoner, is seated opposite him. MUSTAFA's face is badly bruised from the incident in the dining room that day. An officer stands outside the room. Both SHABIR and MUSTAFA have been silent for some time while SHABIR sifts through some paperwork. SHABIR glances at his watch whilst sifting.

MUSTAFA. You must be busy.

SHABIR. Yes.

MUSTAFA. Did it take you long to get here?

SHABIR doesn't respond and continues to sift through the papers.

How did you know?

SHABIR. What happened to your face?

MUSTAFA. Someone tell you?

SHABIR. I'm a solicitor. Believe it or not, word gets round. What happened to your face?

MUSTAFA. Inmate. Think he likes me.

SHABIR. You spoke to them about it?

MUSTAFA glances through the glass at the officer.

MUSTAFA. Yes.

SHABIR. And?

MUSTAFA. They put me in a cell by myself.

...

Didn't expect to see you here. What happened to Peter?

SHABIR. You fired him, apparently. Said you didn't need a solicitor any more because you weren't going to appeal?

...

I'll contact him if you want –

MUSTAFA. No. No, it's okay.

SHABIR. Good, because he wasn't exactly the best man for the case – wasn't exactly unhappy about me taking it off his hands either.

MUSTAFA. Yeah, I guess.

SHABIR. We're going to appeal. Get a sentence reduction if nothing else – but I need more time on this paperwork, sort you out a barrister, a good one this time.

MUSTAFA. What are my chances?

SHABIR. Can't say right now – need some time.

...

MUSTAFA. Who told you?

SHABIR. When did you get back from Pakistan?

MUSTAFA. While ago.

SHABIR. And you didn't think to tell me?

MUSTAFA. Sorry.

SHABIR. Sorry? Is that it? Typical, I don't see you for ages and now this. Look at you, your face, your eyes – have you slept, have you eaten properly?

MUSTAFA. No... But it's okay... Been praying – any time I get, no time for sleep.

SHABIR (*starts gathering the paperwork*).Yeah, well, you need your strength – now more than ever. I'm sure God won't mind if you get a square meal and put in a good night's sleep.

MUSTAFA *is displeased with the last comment, but says nothing.*

MUSTAFA. How are you?

SHABIR *keeps gathering the paperwork and putting it into his briefcase.*

You don't want to be here.

SHABIR. Why didn't you call me? You didn't even think to call me?

MUSTAFA. I don't know. Thought you might be busy.

SHABIR. This is not a joke, Mustafa!

MUSTAFA. I wasn't [joking] –

SHABIR. How the hell do you think I feel when you don't call me to let me know you're back from Pakistan – to tell me you're in court, for God's sake! Instead, I have Malik walking into my office to tell me my brother's been done for manslaughter and *he* thinks I ought to help you with an appeal!

MUSTAFA. Malik came to see you?

SHABIR. Yes. Unannounced. Walked straight into my office – how do you think that looked?

MUSTAFA. I'm sorry.

SHABIR. Stop saying that.

MUSTAFA. But I am. I'm sorry you were embarrassed by the way Malik looked.

SHABIR *could say something but chooses not to, in an attempt to avoid an argument.*

You've been drinking.

SHABIR *stands.*

Because of... this?

SHABIR. I came here to help. You! This is not about me. Nobody survives alone. How many times do I – You just can't... You should have called me.

MUSTAFA. I didn't think you'd come.

SHABIR *closes up his briefcase and goes to the door of the room.*

SHABIR. I'll be back tomorrow.

MUSTAFA. It's good to see you.

SHABIR. Get some sleep.

Lights down.

End of scene.

Scene Three

The next day. A windowless meeting room in the prison – the only window is a small pane on the door. The four walls, two chairs and table are the only features of the room. MUSTAFA *sits alone, his face is still bruised from the incident that took place the day before.* LEN *enters and takes a seat. He has a file with him. He opens it.*

LEN. Right, well, you know why we're here, Mustafa?

...

I'll tell you then, shall I? The incident in the dining hall yesterday?

...

What happened?

MUSTAFA. I don't know.

LEN. You were hurt.

MUSTAFA. Yes.

LEN. If the officers hadn't put a stop to it, you would have been hurt badly.

MUSTAFA. Okay.

LEN. Really? That's okay?

MUSTAFA. Yes.

LEN. Well, that's not the way we feel. In fact, as far as we see it, incidents like this are a sign that things aren't working as well as we'd like. Now, says here that Tony was dining at your table and –

MUSTAFA. My prayer mat's missing.

LEN. – and after passing some comments your way, you pushed his dinner tray – his full dinner tray – into his face.

MUSTAFA. I shouldn't be in there with them.

LEN. And where do you think you should be eating?

MUSTAFA. I don't know. Just not in there.

LEN. There's only one dining area in the prison. I've been here thirty years, don't think that's going to change any time soon. Unless you're thinking of room service?

MUSTAFA. Maybe I should skip mealtimes altogether.

LEN. Right. 'Cept you have to eat something, don't you, Mustafa, to stay alive, I mean. Can't skip mealtimes for ever, can you?

...

Failing that, there is this other option. That you attend mealtimes, have your food, steer clear of any trouble, and leave.

MUSTAFA. I didn't *do* anything.

LEN. Oh, so you didn't do it then? The tray – in his face?

MUSTAFA. No.

LEN. Then I'll ask you again, Mustafa: what happened in the dining room with Tony yesterday?

MUSTAFA. It wasn't me.

LEN. Right. But you were there?

MUSTAFA. Yeah.

LEN. So what happened?

MUSTAFA. Exactly what it says on that piece of paper.

LEN. So you're admitting it?

MUSTAFA. If it says I was sitting there when Tony started chanting 'magic man' at me until his own dinner tray hit him in the face – then, yes, I'm admitting I was there and that's what happened.

LEN. So he threw his own tray up into his face?

MUSTAFA. Yeah, something like that.

LEN. Well, did he or didn't he?

MUSTAFA. It was a full dining hall, Len.

LEN. So why did he lunge at you afterwards?

MUSTAFA. He doesn't like me.

LEN. Try again.

MUSTAFA. I don't know – he was embarrassed?

LEN. Because you'd embarrassed him?

MUSTAFA. Shouldn't you be asking him these questions?

LEN. Do you know why he calls you 'magic man'?

MUSTAFA. My notebook's missing too.

LEN. I think you do. Look, Mustafa, when you got here, no one barely noticed. Quiet as a mouse, no arguments, nothing. Okay, so you still liked to be by yourself, but otherwise everything was fine. What's happened this last week, eh? Where's all this trouble come from?

MUSTAFA. I want my prayer mat back, and my book – why d'you take my book?

LEN. They know what you're in for, and they'll do anything to get a rise out of you.

MUSTAFA. I need my book.

LEN. Which is why I think it would be of benefit if you mixed in more. If you sit in the lotus position in your cell with nothing but your mat and your prayer beads, it'll only feed the rumours and spook stories.

…

Which won't help matters. Do you understand, Mustafa?

MUSTAFA. Yes.

LEN. Good.

MUSTAFA. My prayer mat –

LEN. You know it won't be returned until –

MUSTAFA. It's my prayer mat – I need it to pray five –

LEN. Five times a day, yes, we do know these things. Things have progressed. I understand your faith is important to you – just as our rules and regulations are important to the running of this facility. You know there's the communal quiet room where you can pray in Jamaat with the other Muslim inmates, you can even speak with an imam if you want.

MUSTAFA. I don't want to talk to anyone.

LEN. No, you really don't, do you?

MUSTAFA. I just want to do my time.

…

LEN. Good answer, Mustafa. Normally that'd be music to my ears. But, like I said, this last week I've had more conversations about you than any other inmate. (*Looks through file*.) Incident in the washrooms –

MUSTAFA. That wasn't me. Look, when do I get my things?

LEN. – several incidents in the dining room –

MUSTAFA. I told you, they don't like me.

LEN. – fight broke out during exercise.

MUSTAFA. That wasn't me.

LEN. Right. But it's a long list. See what I'm getting at? You've been moved to a single cell recently but that is not a long-term solution.

MUSTAFA. Are you going to give me my things back?

LEN. We have a system based on earned privileges, as you know by now. Following an incident like yesterday, those privileges will be taken away.

MUSTAFA. My prayer mat is not a 'privilege', it's a necessity.

LEN. Now, I've just outlined the other option for prayer – so I want to be clear that you understand that we are not preventing you from praying. But you can't spend the whole time in your cell. You need to shower, and exercise and eat.

And if there's trouble every time you step out of that cell, then we need to talk about it.

MUSTAFA. They don't like me, I told you. If you don't like it then keep me in my cell.

LEN. And you'd like that, wouldn't you, son?

MUSTAFA. That's the best I can do. Best for everyone.

…

LEN. This is your first time inside and I know some inmates find it difficult at first – close themselves off. But you don't talk to anyone, you don't interact –

MUSTAFA. I need to practise certain elements of my faith. It's important. I couldn't do it in a shared cell with an inmate. It requires concentration and privacy –

LEN. If you wanted twenty-four-hour privacy, Mustafa, you should have kept out of prison. And I really hope you're not trying to tell me that you've caused these incidents in order to be placed in a single cell?

…

Some officers have noticed that you're not eating at mealtimes.

MUSTAFA. That why you searched my cell?

LEN. If you're not eating any of the food provided by the prison, then naturally we want to know what you're surviving on. Inmates are not permitted any non-prison food.

MUSTAFA. And did you find anything? Aside from my edible prayer mat?

LEN. Well, you're not wasting away yet, you've got to be living off something. (*Closes file, laughs.*) 'Edible prayer mat'… I'm not against you, Mustafa. I'm trying to help. Whatever it is you do, it makes the inmates jittery.

MUSTAFA. I keep telling you I don't –

LEN. Nervous, volatile inmates make nervous prison staff. You want to serve your time in peace – we're here to help you do that. (*Stands.*) We provide halal food options, communal prayer facilities – there are plenty of ways to spend your

time in here without having to send fellow inmates to
healthcare.

MUSTAFA. What about Tony?

LEN. Let us worry about him.

MUSTAFA. I mean, is he okay?

LEN. Few injuries to his face. Few stains on his prison clothes
and his ego – nothing that won't wash out. Good to see
you're concerned – I hope that means you don't hold a
grudge.

*LEN is ready to end the meeting, but he starts to look a little
uncomfortable – agitated – as if the room is getting
uncomfortably warm. He unbuttons his collar. The lights in
the room begin to flicker. It's barely noticeable at first.*

Yesterday's antics buys both of you some time in individual
cells to cool off. Don't look so pleased, Mustafa. Keep
yourself to yourself all the time and the rumours and
names'll only spread.

MUSTAFA. What about my prayer mat and things?

*LEN's discomfort increases. The lights flicker, more
noticeably. MUSTAFA looks up at the lighting tube but LEN
doesn't seem to notice. He stands with the file, ready to
leave. MUSTAFA unwinds his tasbih (prayer beads) from
his wrist and holds it in the palm of his hand. LEN moves to
the door, intending to indicate to the officer outside that the
meeting is over.*

LEN *(heading to the door)*. In the meantime, it might be an idea
to get involved with some of the activities. Guv sees you're
in the rec room, sees you're seeing visitors, staying out of
trouble, might be good for you.

MUSTAFA. I don't have any visitors.

LEN. Not true – there's a Mr Malik who's been requesting
visits since you came in.

MUSTAFA. I don't want to talk to anyone.

*LEN wants to leave the room but something is keeping him
there. The lights flicker off completely for a fraction of a
moment and then return to full brightness. LEN gestures*

*through the door to the officer outside – five more minutes.
He turns and faces the prisoner. Something about the way he
looks at* MUSTAFA *is different.*

LEN. How do you know, hmm? Maybe this Mr Malik has got
something to say, how do you know it isn't something you
want to hear? You know I can't force you, but like they used
to say in the old BT ads, Mustafa, 'it's good to talk'…

MUSTAFA. Mr Malik is the victim's father, Len.

LEN. Sorry?

MUSTAFA. Mr Malik, he's the dead boy's father.

LEN *almost smiles, it's unnerving. He walks slowly back to
the table. As he walks, we see he no longer moves like* LEN.
*He seems different somehow, the change is small but
noticeable. He is no longer agitated.*

LEN. Oh. You sure?

MUSTAFA. Am I sure?

LEN. I mean, you sure it's *that* Mr Malik?

MUSTAFA. Yes.

LEN. And why do you think he wants to see you?

MUSTAFA. Look, I just don't want any visitors.

LEN *slaps the prisoner across the face, hard.* MUSTAFA
*tumbles off the chair, he falls to the floor knocking the chair
over. Fresh blood slips from a wound* MUSTAFA *suffered at
the hands of Tony the previous day. When* LEN *speaks now,
the manner of his speech has changed; he seems arrogant
and displeased with* MUSTAFA, *like a master who's
displeased with his servant.*

LEN. I think I know what he wants to say. Shall I hazard a
guess, eh, Mustafa? Maybe he wants to thank you for giving
him one less mouth to feed, eh? Maybe he wants to bring
you some wholesome home-cooked food from pretty little
wifey that you *will* eat! Or maybe he wants to lick your face,
put his hand deep, deep inside your throat and rip out your
guts for what you did!

LEN *looks furious enough to strike* MUSTAFA *again.*
Instead, he takes a handkerchief out of his pocket and shoves
it into the prisoner's hand. He gets up and turns away from
MUSTAFA.

Get up.

MUSTAFA *gets up off the floor. The beads on his tasbih*
keep turning as he continues to recite a dua (prayer) in his
mind while he talks to LEN. MUSTAFA *addresses the officer*
more carefully now.

MUSTAFA. You're angry.

LEN *is silent, with his back to* MUSTAFA.

There's no trouble, like you said.

LEN. Yeah.

MUSTAFA. No one here wants any trouble.

LEN. Oh no, some people like trouble, they thrive off it…
magic man… (*Laughs.*) You, magic man? They ain't seen
nothing yet. Like Tony… (*Laughs.*) Listen to you asking if
he's okay, aren't you pleased he got hurt?

MUSTAFA. What do you want?

LEN. You know what I want. (*Turns to face* MUSTAFA *and*
speaks softly, casually.) I want you to open your eyes and
look around you… You're one of many inmates – you're like
a mouse in a cage, Mustafa. Scurrying around in a cage,
being told when to wash, when to sleep, when to wake, when
to eat and when to shit. Oh, I see your arrogance. You think
you can beat me, you think you can actually…? Well, you
don't want to upset me – I'm an old man, with an old ticker,
Mustafa, too much excitement might not be good for me.
Never know what might happen…

DAN *enters, clocks the fallen chair.*

(*To* DAN.) Get him out of here, we're done.

DAN *leads* MUSTAFA *out of the room, the prisoner is*
watching LEN *as he is led out.*

Ask the kitchen to get him something, think he might be
hungry.

Alone in the room, LEN *stands where he is for a moment. The arrogance drains from his face and is replaced with a vague confused expression. He moves methodically and replaces the chair in its original position. He sits in it and lays his head on the table. A moment passes before* DAN *enters.*

DAN. Terry's got him. Everything all right?

LEN (*raising head*). Yeah… yeah… everything's fine.

DAN. 'S just…

LEN. What?

DAN. The chair. Did something happen?

LEN. Oh yeah, come to think of it, something did happen. He got up too quick and knocked the chair over. You wanna fill in the paperwork?

DAN. Oh… right. You sure everything's all right? Only, you don't look so well?

LEN. I'm fine.

DAN. Right… cos I was, you know, thinking that maybe…

LEN. What?

DAN. It's just they've put me down for the weekend. Only I forgot Pam's got this do – her cousin or something – anyway, I gotta be there and no one else wants to cover.

LEN. And?

DAN. Please, Len.

LEN. Can't help, mate, working the same shift as you.

DAN. I know, but… could you have a word with Chris for me? He'll listen to you.

LEN. Have a word with him yourself.

DAN. Len? Come on, you know I can't let Pam down, I mean, she'll go mad if she thinks I forgot.

LEN. But you did forget, you idiot.

DAN. Right, so you're just gonna let me get it in the neck, are you?

LEN. I said get lost.

DAN (*closes the door*). No, I gotta sort this out – or she's gonna find out that I'm down for a shift and then all hell'll break loose. Come on, Len, why you being like this? Look, I won't say anything about this, I swear.

LEN. About what?

DAN. Mustafa – you, the chair…

LEN *looks around the room – he seems increasingly to have no recollection of exactly what just took place with* MUSTAFA.

LEN. Nothing happened.

DAN. Okay, if you say so, Len.

LEN. It's work – she'll understand.

DAN. No she won't.

LEN. It'll do you good to make a stand.

DAN. And what the fuck does that mean?

LEN. Means you're working the weekend.

LEN *stands, wavers, and then falls back into the chair.*

DAN. You sure you're all right?

LEN. Yeah, just…

DAN. It's that magic man – guy's got some kind of weird shit going on. You shouldn't have been alone with him.

LEN. Shut up, Dan, just need to have my lunch, that's all. Give me a minute, will you.

DAN. Shall I get someone?

LEN. No. Just give me a minute. Alone.

DAN *pulls the second chair up close to* LEN *and sits down.*

DAN. Well?

LEN. What?

DAN. Did he spill?… About Tony?

LEN. Oh, do you ever stop?

DAN. What, I'm serious – did he?

LEN. Get back to work.

DAN. About yesterday, Len… I was right there when –

LEN. Yes, yes, you said!

DAN (*comes closer*). Thing is, magic Mustafa didn't touch Tony's tray. It was in Tony's hands when it smashed him in the face.

LEN. So why didn't you say so?

DAN. I tried! You wouldn't let me.

LEN (*not totally convinced*). So, Tony did it to himself.

DAN. Tony? He's OCD about his gear and his clothes and his things – you telling me he'd smack a full dinner tray into his own face – in front of everyone?

LEN. Yeah.

DAN. Wha– come on, Len – why would he?

LEN. What's the alternative?

DAN.…

LEN. Eh?

DAN.…

LEN. There is no alternative, Dan. Tony'd probably have done it just to get Mustafa in trouble – or to try and make out the 'magic man' thing has got legs. And you and the other officers believing all the stories – like you're on some Scouts' camping trip – are not helping matters. *Comprende?*

DAN. All right, all right, calm down, man.

LEN. Get back to work.

DAN *exits.* LEN *sits, he feels something in the hand he used to strike* MUSTAFA. *He flexes his fingers and stares at them.*

End of scene.

Scene Four

It is late on the same day. MUSTAFA*'s cell.* DAN *enters the corridor outside the cell.* MUSTAFA *has been praying on a blanket – his prayer mat not yet returned. He has finished his namaz and is making dua.*

DAN. Everything okay, Mustafa, eh? Happy now you got a cell to yourself? How come you don't pray in Jamaat – like the rest of 'em? Thought you were meant to – you know, the blokes.

MUSTAFA *finishes his dua and looks at* DAN.

(*Pleased with himself.*) Yeah… see, I know about Muslims – Mo's been telling me, you know, young lad, always in the quiet room?

MUSTAFA *gets up and folds the blanket and places it on the end of the bed.* DAN *is staring at him.*

MUSTAFA. Something bothering you, Dan?

DAN. You, Mustafa, always you… How comes you're praying on that?

MUSTAFA. Someone's taken my prayer mat.

DAN. Oh yeah, right.

MUSTAFA. My things?

DAN. Sorry, mate, that's down to your personal officer and Len's gone off sick.

MUSTAFA*'s interest is sparked.*

First time in a hundred years probably. Never goes off sick, does Len. That's why they got me covering for him – gotta check on you, haven't I?

MUSTAFA. He okay?

DAN. Dunno, mate. Looked a bit peaky – but I'm sure he'll be fine.

MUSTAFA. Maybe you should call him.

DAN. What?

MUSTAFA. Maybe you should call him, check he's okay.

DAN. Well, thanks for the advice, Muzz, but I think I'll let him rest.

MUSTAFA. When will he be back?

DAN. Mind your own.

MUSTAFA. I need my things.

DAN. Do you now?…Yeah, I saw him after he had his one-to-one with you this morning – about Tony. Pretty much peaky from the minute you left. Mind you, you didn't look too pretty either. Funny that, eh? Something happen – in the meeting?

MUSTAFA *settles on the floor, cross-legged with his tasbih in his hand.*

Round and round it goes, eh, Muzz, little beads in your hand. What you doing? You putting a curse on me or something? Only, I was in there the other day and I saw a circle on the floor. D'you make that?

MUSTAFA. Must have been here from before.

DAN. Been talking to Mo – you know. Said you got a genie… Got it out of that boy and now you use it to protect yourself – like a spooky bodyguard or something.

MUSTAFA *doesn't take the bait.*

(*Closer to the bars.*) Go on then, tell me what happened?

MUSTAFA. Hm?

DAN. With Len, why's he off?

MUSTAFA. You're the one who spoke to him – last I saw him –

DAN. Don't mess me about, go on, tell me – or tell me about Tony, how did you do it? D'you psych 'em up – that it? You do a Derren Brown and then they go berserk and kick off?

…

Oi?

MUSTAFA. I don't do anything.

DAN. Ah, for fuck's sake – I thought you were gonna spill 'n' all!

MUSTAFA. I just did.

DAN (*under his breath*). Freak. (*Louder.*) I'm watching you.

MUSTAFA. But do you ever listen, Dan?

DAN. Careful, Mustafa, I ain't a soft touch like our Len.

MUSTAFA *regards* DAN *more closely now – suspecting he may not be himself – as with* LEN *earlier.*

MUSTAFA. No, course not.

...

DAN. So if it ain't you – who is it? Is it that genie of yours? He in there with you now, is he?

MUSTAFA. What do you think?

DAN. I think you're playing games. Mo said you cured him.

MUSTAFA. What?

DAN. Yeah, said he had some trouble or other – with his wife, I think he said – and you fixed it for him. What did you fix, eh, fix it so she wasn't trouble for him no more, did ya...

MUSTAFA. I spoke to him, that's all.

DAN. Nah. Don't buy it. He said you knew things about him, about his wife. Said you drew a chart an' everything... worked it all out for him.

MUSTAFA. Mo's got a big mouth.

DAN. Yeah, or maybe I have my ways of making him talk...

MUSTAFA. He has nightmares.

DAN. What?

MUSTAFA. Mo. He has nightmares, about his wife, his kids – you know what he's in for?

DAN. Oh yeah, I know what everyone's in for... Set his house on fire with his family still in it, didn't he? Crazy fuck.

MUSTAFA. He's not crazy. I just helped him with his nightmares, that's all.

DAN. What, no magic?

MUSTAFA. No, Dan.

DAN. Well, that's a disappointment. Why don't you tell me something, eh – sort me out?

MUSTAFA. Nothing to sort.

DAN is quiet for a moment.

DAN. See, thing is, Mustafa, I'm pissed off. I'm already having trouble finding cover for my weekend, so having to work tonight… Way I figure it, least you can do is help the night along a little?

MUSTAFA gets up and stands by the cell bars in front of DAN. DAN takes half a step back.

MUSTAFA. Give me your hands.

DAN. You what?

MUSTAFA. Give me your hands and I'll tell you what I know.

DAN thinks for a moment – he's alone, but the cell door is locked – so he tentatively puts one hand through the bars. MUSTAFA takes it, calmly. He holds it firm with a finger on DAN's wrist.

DAN. What the hell are [you doing] –

MUSTAFA is quiet for a moment. When DAN's discomfort increases, he lets go of his hand and returns to his seated position on the floor of the cell.

Well?

MUSTAFA. You have an ulcer.

DAN. Yeah, how… Oh, I get it – (*Laughs.*) That's clever that is – you must have heard me complaining – seen me taking those fruity tablet thingies.

MUSTAFA. It's stress-related.

DAN. Well, it don't take a genius to work that one out.

MUSTAFA. What's causing the stress, Dan?

DAN. Ain't that what you're meant to tell me?

MUSTAFA. I can, but I don't think you want to hear it from me.

DAN. Oi, I can take it.

MUSTAFA. Can you?

...

It'll only get worse if you don't deal with the problem.

DAN. I ain't got a problem. You're the freak with the problem.

MUSTAFA. Then, like I said, you've got nothing to sort out.

DAN. Yeah, yeah, that's right. Lights out at eleven.

DAN exits. MUSTAFA watches as he goes, and keeps his gaze on the door for a long moment. When he's sure DAN's gone, he takes some chalk from his pocket and draws a circle around himself where he is sitting on the floor. He sits as one would during Salaat and begins reciting silently.

End of scene.

Scene Five

The following day. Recreation room. In a nearby space, we hear a football-match commentary and a large group of prisoners watching the game and responding to the action on the pitch. MUSTAFA stands alone in front of a pool table, playing a round by himself. He does not use the white ball to pot the rest, but seems to be making the game up as he goes along. He looks uncomfortable – like he's trying to look normal. LEN approaches.

LEN. Well, guv, the good news is Mustafa spent some time outside his cell. Bad news is he's playing by himself. You not into the footy?

MUSTAFA. No.

LEN. Not into pool either, I see – Mustafa, you're supposed to hit the white ball and pocket the others!

MUSTAFA. Got to do something to get my things back, right?

LEN puts MUSTAFA's prayer mat and notebook on the table. The book is old and well used, with notes on protruding loose leaves tucked amongst the pages.

Thank you.

MUSTAFA *slides the book and mat towards himself – visibly relieved to have his items returned.*

LEN. S'pose you deserve it – for showing willing.

MUSTAFA *plays and doesn't respond.*

You're still not eating much, from what I hear –

MUSTAFA. I don't like the smell in there.

LEN (*laughs*). Well, neither do most of 'em, mate – but they ain't getting the Febreze out just for you. In and out, that's all it takes. Eat whatever it is you're sneaking in here, but pretend it's their shit you're surviving on.

MUSTAFA. What, you're not going to ransack my cell in search for WMDs again?

LEN. No. Frankly I don't know how you're doing it – pretty impressive really – and don't tell anyone I said that.

MUSTAFA. You still think I'm eating from a secret stash?

LEN. Like I've been telling the guv – you're living off something.

MUSTAFA. Water, and prayer.

LEN. That right? Tough diet, don't think I could do it. Don't look like you're sleeping much either.

MUSTAFA. I'm fasting, Len. Helps me... focus. I need to focus, 'specially now.

LEN. But it's not Ramadan.

MUSTAFA. Doesn't have to be. Brings you closer to God, fasting.

LEN. Each to his own.

    ...

MUSTAFA. I see what you're thinking.

LEN. Mind-reader an' all now?

MUSTAFA. You're wondering how I could get closer to God after what I've done.

LEN *does not respond.*

You know, I hated fasting when I was a kid. Didn't get it.
Why would anyone think it'd be good for you to not eat or
drink...? Even cheated sometimes.

LEN. Must say, I never got my head round that one either.

MUSTAFA. Once when I was older, it's Ramzaan and I'm in a
shop trying to buy dates and get home to break fast with my
brother and this old guy's with his grandson and he's holding
up the queue. First he wants a few more items, then he's lost
his wallet, then he remembers something else he needs – and
he doesn't speak a word of English. He's Bengali, going on in
his own language and the kid on the till, Pakistani kid, is too
embarrassed to try and communicate with the old guy. So I
storm to the front of the queue and I start yelling at the old
guy and shouting at the kid on the till. I've been waiting ages,
it's boiling hot and there's like a massive hole in my stomach
growling for food, for water, for this old guy to get out of the
way! I've got to get home, I'm telling them, to break fast!

LEN. Fasting in the summer, can't be easy, son.

MUSTAFA. Kid behind the till just gets more embarrassed,
takes my money, hands me the dates and I leave. Got home,
too late despite my efforts. My aunt's yelling about me
getting the wrong kinda dates, my brother's nowhere to be
seen so I leave – still haven't eaten anything. I'm walking
down the road in a rage, hungry as hell, and I see the old
Bengali guy sitting on the street with his grandson. They
obviously didn't get out of the shop too soon so they're
breaking their fast right there in the street. The kid's smiling
and the old guy's feeding him a banana and an apple – they
didn't have much. I see this tired old Bengali guy, in the
boiling heat after a fifteen-hour fast, sipping water patiently,
while his grandson eats the only thing they've got before
they walk home. The kid's too young to fast – was eating
chocolate in the shop but still he's munching away at the
fruit – asking his gramps for more water. He sees me and...
I'm ashamed – don't know why. So I look away, think I'm
gonna cross over the road, keep walking. But the kid runs up
and pulls me over – the old guy's telling me to sit. And he
gives me a date, and a sip of water – pats me on the back,
like he knows how angry and hungry I am. He offers me the
fruit... Three of us sat there, on a pavement in the middle of

the city sharing an apple, a banana and handful of dates. I haven't missed a fast since that day.

…

Thing is, Len, everyone in that queue – Granddad included – was fasting. All of us were hungry. Everyone was boiling. I'd been fasting for years and I never thought about that – ridiculous, I know. My brother, who I rushed home for? Wasn't fasting, out with his college mates somewhere in the city centre. That was it then. I wanted to know how an old guy like that, who must have been more knackered and hungry than me when I was shouting into his face in the shop – could smile and offer me a fair share at his meal when he had every right to kick off. Sometimes you have to do things for someone else – when you know you're going to get nothing back but trouble. Just cos it's the right thing to do… It ain't just about the food and drink, Len, it's about who we are, from sunup to sundown. Who we want to be…

LEN. Do you know that's the most I've heard you say since you've been in here? Typical – the one time you want to talk and it's about religion.

MUSTAFA. Not for you?

LEN. I had a lot of philosophers and preachers in here over the years, Mustafa. I learned a long time ago that this, this planet, this life, it's all we got – need to make the most of it.

MUSTAFA. So you've never believed?

LEN. Only in what I know. What you can see, hear, witness. All the other stuff… well, it's just smoke and mirrors – no offence.

MUSTAFA. You've never experienced something outside of that – something you can't explain?

LEN. No.

MUSTAFA. Must be a nice place, knowing everything's a surety.

LEN (*less sure*). Yeah…

MUSTAFA. So you spend that one precious life working in here?

LEN. Well, I guess you got to give something back, eh.

MUSTAFA. Sounds like you're feeling better.

LEN. Eh?

MUSTAFA. Dan said you were off sick yesterday afternoon.

LEN glances around the empty room.

LEN. Yeah, yeah, just felt a bit off – getting old. Better now. One day closer to retirement.

MUSTAFA. Good.

...

LEN. How's your face healing up?

MUSTAFA. Like a peach.

LEN. Listen, Mustafa, our last meeting... everything okay?

MUSTAFA. Yep.

LEN. Nothing... you want to say?

MUSTAFA. No. You?

LEN. Nope. Everything going okay with your solicitor?

MUSTAFA. Yeah, why – have you heard something?

LEN. No, just making conversation, Mustafa – that's the next step once you've mastered the pool table, chit-chat.

MUSTAFA. Right.

LEN. Look, if you decided you wanted another personal officer, I can have a word.

MUSTAFA. Why?

In the other room, the prisoners jeer at the telly.

LEN. I'm just saying if you wanted to, if maybe you felt I didn't handle things... right.

MUSTAFA. Okay.

LEN waits as if for a response, MUSTAFA concentrates on the pool table.

LEN. So we're all right then?

MUSTAFA. Yeah.

LEN. Good.

> LEN *starts to walk towards the room where the prisoners are watching the match.*

MUSTAFA. He's my brother.

> LEN *stops.*

LEN. Sorry?

MUSTAFA. My solicitor, he's also my older brother, the one who thinks he's going to get me an appeal.

LEN. Right. Well, that's good?

MUSTAFA. You think?

LEN. It isn't about what I think.

MUSTAFA. Yeah, well, he hasn't turned up today, so maybe it's not so good.

LEN. Right.

MUSTAFA. Len, if you wanted to get me another personal officer, if you'd rather it wasn't you, that's fine.

> LEN *approaches* MUSTAFA *again.*

LEN. I been working in this prison for thirty years, son, never turned my back on an inmate yet. Best part of the job – trying to help you guys get out better than you came in.

MUSTAFA. No matter what we're in for?

LEN. I leave the judges and juries to worry about that. I'm always telling the new officers – if you look at the crime instead of the man it doesn't make the job any easier, quite the opposite actually.

MUSTAFA. Think you can do that for me? See beyond my crime?

LEN. Well, that's probably down to you as much as me. But I take my job serious, Mustafa – like to do things right, you know – always have. If… If some day I didn't… I'd want to face up to it.

MUSTAFA. Course.

LEN. Yeah… As you were, then… Better go see if we've scored. Oh, and guv called me in. They're thinking about sending you to the vulnerable-prisoner unit.

MUSTAFA. Does that mean I'd be in with a cellmate?

LEN. Probably.

MUSTAFA. Len –

LEN. I recommended you stay in isolation for the time being, for your own good. Told him we could manage it.

MUSTAFA. Thank you.

LEN. Don't thank me, son, it won't be for ever. And maybe you should try and use the white ball to pot the others. Might come out of here a pool champ if nothing else.

End of scene.

Scene Six

Same day. MUSTAFA*'s cell. Night, lights-out. On the table, the notebook* LEN *returned to* MUSTAFA *is open, with some loose leaves lying nearby. There is a dim light from the corridor and a high window.* MUSTAFA *sits inside a hisar (chalk circle) on the floor. His eyes are closed. He has his tasbih in his hand.* DAN *enters the corridor outside the cell, switches the lights on. They are bright, but every so often they flicker. He has a clipboard with him.*

DAN. You up?

He taps the clipboard on the bars.

Visitation request, thought you might like to sign it before I head off. (*Looking at clipboard.*) Mr Malik… Mr Abdul Malik. Recognise him? Come and take a look.

MUSTAFA*'s eyes remain closed.*

MUSTAFA. It's a bit late for that, isn't it?

DAN. Guv thinks it'd be good for you to have a visitor. I want you to see him – I want to see him.

MUSTAFA. No.

DAN. No? Sad really… you kill a man's son and he wants to see you. Surely he deserves to have his request approved? Come here and take a look.

The lights flicker – DAN is outside the cell and then, after a flicker, inside. He looks displeased and has the same manner and movement as LEN had in the meeting in which he struck MUSTAFA. DAN walks right up to MUSTAFA but stops at the outer edge of the chalk circle. MUSTAFA's eyes remain closed.

What, you don't trust me? What's the world coming to if there's no trust, eh?

MUSTAFA. I see you.

DAN. Do you?

MUSTAFA. I see you.

DAN. Maybe you should step out of there and come get a closer look.

MUSTAFA. Or you could step in – it's just a bit of chalk, right, Dan…?

DAN laughs, knowingly.

Why are you here?

DAN. You called me, remember?

MUSTAFA. Why are you still here?

DAN. I just want to talk to you, about the boy.

MUSTAFA. It's time for you to leave.

DAN. But I've only just started to enjoy myself. Didn't you miss me? Come on, you can be honest, there's only you and me here. How did it feel, huh, I bet you weren't expecting that now, were you? (*Sitting on the bed.*) Poor little Mustafa, accepting his punishment for a bad, bad thing… Thought you'd done it all and now you just had to wait out your time…? You didn't honestly think you could get rid of me that easily?

…

Thing is, this isolation business, spoiling my fun, isn't it. You should get out more, interact with the locals… I like them…

MUSTAFA. Go back to where you came from.

DAN *laughs*.

DAN. Heard that loads, didn't you, eh, when you and your brother came over here… (*Jeers*.) *Pakis! Go back to where you came from!* Two little orphan infants making their way in the big bad world together… But look at the two of you now… not together any more. He's nice, your brother. Nothing like you. Well dressed, well spoken. Pissed as anything that he had to come here, to see you.

MUSTAFA. Leave him out of it. I'm giving you a chance to go, now.

DAN. Is he any good, Shabir? Be great if he gets us off – we can get back out there, plenty to see and do. We could pay old Malik a visit. Yes, I like that. We could go see Mr ·Malik… Mrs Malik… and Miss…

MUSTAFA. Enough!

DAN. What's her name again, the boy's little sister…? She was pretty…

MUSTAFA *opens his eyes*.

MUSTAFA. I said enough!

DAN. Thing is, Mustafa – Shabir isn't here because he cares about you… He's here because his partners back at the firm don't like you.

MUSTAFA. No.

DAN. He's spitting fire at the thought that dirty little Malik came knocking on his door to tell him to help you. He doesn't want anything to do with you – with what you've done. He hates you for it.

MUSTAFA. You're a parasite, a leech who sucks the life out of innocent people for –

DAN. Remember, you need to be nice to me. Can you do that, Mustafa, huh, be nice? You take the boy away from me, so where you go, I go. You made it that way. Not always good to get what you want, is it?

MUSTAFA. I want you to leave this place and never –

DAN. Shame your little plan went awry – tried to rid the world of me, save the boy, but look what happened…

MUSTAFA. What do you want?

DAN (*enraged*). You took the boy from me! (*Calms himself.*) You took the boy from me. And still I'm good to you. Anyone, I mean anyone, even looks at you in this place and I sort them out, don't I?

MUSTAFA. Do not pretend to be my friend.

DAN. Oh no. No, no, you misunderstand, Mustafa. You see, I could never let anyone hurt you… That's *my* job…

DAN *leans forward now, as close to* MUSTAFA *as he can without entering the hisar.*

MUSTAFA. Go or I will end you!

DAN (*laughs heartily*). Oooh… you sound angry… or is that scared? Reminds me of someone… can you guess who?

MUSTAFA. Show yourself – your real self, don't hide behind these people.

DAN. You couldn't take it.

MUSTAFA (*holds the taveez around his neck*). I have Allah's Kalaam to protect me – show yourself!

DAN. All in good time… I want you to see the boy's father –

MUSTAFA. No.

DAN *is ready to strike* MUSTAFA – *but the hisar prevents him.*

DAN. I want you to see him, his wife – and his daughter. His beautiful, young, ripe daughter –

MUSTAFA. You sick –

DAN. Careful, anger means weakness, you know that as well as I do. I want the girl.

MUSTAFA. You will never go near them again!

DAN. She's the only replacement for the boy and you know it, you owe it to me!

MUSTAFA. Do you hear? Never!

DAN. Listen to yourself, Mustafa – magic Mustafa – didn't think twice about sacrificing the boy –

MUSTAFA. That's not what happened!

DAN. Using him to practise your pathetic games.

MUSTAFA. Malik asked me to help his son –

DAN. Bet he regrets it –

MUSTAFA. Why are you here?

DAN. I want you to –

MUSTAFA. Why?!

> MUSTAFA *stands in a rage, almost stepping out of the hisar.*

DAN. Come on… just… one… more… step.

MUSTAFA. Why?…

DAN. Come on, Mustafa, you know you want to.

…

MUSTAFA. You can't leave…

DAN. We can do this again, but you will lose. That's the thing about you, people, you never learn… No one believes you, Mustafa – no one sees, no one hears, no one remembers…

> MUSTAFA *sits, closes his eyes tight – and starts to recite to himself, rocking back and forth like a child learning Qur'ān in a madrasa; the tasbih held tightly in his hand.* DAN *faces the audience. The flickering of the lights increases, becoming more erratic.* DAN's *voice changes to that of the seventeen-year-old boy. His face is angry, then emotional and then scared. The fear stays and grows. As* MUSTAFA *prays in the background, the boy breathes heavy, deep, fearful breaths that are too loud to be natural. And then he screams.* MUSTAFA *is shaken out of his prayer, he looks at* DAN, *who speaks in the boy's voice.*

> (*Desperate.*) Help… help me… please… Mustafa… Just… make it stop, Mustafa… make it stop… help me… (*Screams.*) PLEASE!

The sounds are a brutal reminder of another time and place, an action replay. DAN*'s panic-stricken breath turns to steady, shallow breathing; and the tears turn to a quiet, sinister grin.*

Made you look.

The lights flicker. In a moment, DAN *is gone.* MUSTAFA *is alone. The lights go out.*

End of scene.

Scene Seven

The next day. MUSTAFA *sits in the same glass room as before. He looks tired from his encounter with 'DAN' the previous night.* SHABIR *does not have a tie on today, his collar is undone, and his jacket is over his arm when he enters the room. He puts his jacket and case down and remains standing.*

SHABIR. Okay, so we got off on the wrong foot the other day. I'm sorry if it was anything I said. I appreciate it can't be easy in here... it must be... Anyway, I'm sorry it's taken longer than I said to come back.

   ...

Mustafa?

MUSTAFA. How's your wife?

SHABIR. She's... good, she's fine, thanks, thanks for asking.

   ...

Look, this is all nice, you and me and this. But, bottom line, it isn't going to help us get you out of here.

MUSTAFA. I don't think they let murderers go that easy, Shabir.

SHABIR. Manslaughter. You've been convicted and sentenced for manslaughter with diminished responsibility. Unless you're telling me something new?

MUSTAFA. A boy died. Whatever they call it, whatever terms you use...

SHABIR. These aren't terms, Mustafa, it's the law.
Manslaughter with diminished responsibility – fourteen
years – do you know what that means?

…

You look worse than last time. Have you slept?

MUSTAFA. No. Had a… visitor.

SHABIR. Who? Malik?

MUSTAFA. No. Forget it. Look, I never intended to get you
mixed up in this.

SHABIR. Well, that's the thing about family, isn't it; intend it,
don't intend, it makes no difference.

MUSTAFA. Why are you here?

SHABIR. What? I told you, Malik asked me –

MUSTAFA. I mean, why did you come. When you found out?

SHABIR. Isn't it obvious?

…

MUSTAFA. They giving you a hard time at work?

SHABIR. Look, we need to –

MUSTAFA. Are they?

SHABIR. I'm a partner. While you were away, I… I'm a
partner at the firm now.

MUSTAFA. Congratulations.

SHABIR. One with a brother who's been convicted of killing
some kid during an exorcism. Congratulations are… pointless.

MUSTAFA. That's why you're here.

SHABIR. What difference does it make?

MUSTAFA. A lot. To me.

SHABIR. Wish you'd have stayed in Pakistan. Mind you, I
don't know what you were up to over there.

MUSTAFA. Training, I guess.

SHABIR. Oh, for heaven's sake – you weren't... Please don't tell me you were up some mountain with a Kalashnikov!

MUSTAFA. Ibadat – I was learning under Amil Zahid Hus[sain] –

SHABIR. Oh, that would be right. I should have known, minute you hit the ground I bet you were off in some cave meditating with nothing but your tasbih and a –

MUSTAFA. Don't do this.

SHABIR. Why? A boy is dead, just like you said.

MUSTAFA. Yes.

SHABIR. There are people out there who are mourning your sentence, thinking you *saved* this boy from some... some...

MUSTAFA. Djinn. You can't even say it... And what do the others think? Some people think I'm a hero, and the others...?

SHABIR. Think you're a crazed Mullah who killed a boy who may have suffered from a mental disorder.

MUSTAFA *gets up and kicks back his chair.* SHABIR *nods through the glass to an unseen officer, indicating everything is okay.*

MUSTAFA. If you think that then you really shouldn't be [here] –

SHABIR. That's not what I said.

MUSTAFA. But it's what you're thinking.

SHABIR. Is it?

...

MUSTAFA (*pointing*). There.

SHABIR (*looking down at his body*). What?

MUSTAFA. That vein on your neck. It's twitching. Always twitches when you're nervous.

SHABIR. I'm not nerv[ous] –

MUSTAFA. Yeah you are. You're trying to convince me to appeal when you don't believe I should.

SHABIR. What I am doing is acting as your legal representative.

MUSTAFA. How much did you have to drink before you came here?

SHABIR. What?

MUSTAFA. How much – surely, as your client, I deserve to know?

...

Don't look now, but it's twitching.

SHABIR. Fuck you.

...

MUSTAFA. Here's the thing, Shabir. Some people think I'm a hero and some people think I'm a murderer. But they're all out there living their lives and I'm in here. Alone. And there's nothing you can do about it.

SHABIR. I can get a sentence reduction. I know I can.

...

SHABIR *grabs his bag and empties some files onto the table.*

Tell me what happened.

MUSTAFA. You've read the files.

SHABIR. I want to know from you first.

MUSTAFA. I can't do this...

SHABIR. Everything. Start with the boy.

This is it, make or break.

SHABIR *gestures for* MUSTAFA *to sit. He does so. This isn't going to be easy for him, but he sits.*

MUSTAFA. He wasn't just some kid. You know him. Kamran. I taught him Qur'ān from maybe four, five years old.

SHABIR. I remember.

MUSTAFA. He wanted to be a Hafiz but his mum wasn't up for it.

SHABIR. Because of you?

MUSTAFA. Because it meant his secular education would take a back seat and she didn't want that. Didn't want the Qur'ān to take up space in his mind that GCSE Biology might need... I stopped teaching him when he was about eight, he was a quick learner, finished the Qur'ān about three times while he was with me. But I still saw him around after that, saw his dad.

SHABIR. Malik.

MUSTAFA. Yeah. Lived close by for years, saw them all the time...

SHABIR. So when this... happened, he was seventeen?

MUSTAFA. Yes. I went to Pakistan, was there for a year, maybe more. When I got back, I didn't see Malik or Kamran. Heard people talking about them, though, saying the boy had lost weight, lost his hair... They said he was possessed.

SHABIR. So you went to see him?

MUSTAFA. No, I prayed for him. Then one day, Malik comes to my door. He was in a state. He wanted me to come and see his son – he'd only just heard I was back.

SHABIR. And...?

MUSTAFA. He wasn't the boy I remembered. Was older, of course, but smaller – least, it seemed like it. Weak, thin, pulled half his hair out – bitten the inside of his cheeks out...

SHABIR. Had they been to a doctor?

MUSTAFA. Didn't ask.

SHABIR. But –

MUSTAFA. I'm not a physician – that's not why I was there. He'd been like that for over a year apparently. Whole family was... sad, burdened. House was black with smoke in places. They hadn't bothered to fix it, paint it.

SHABIR. Smoke?

MUSTAFA. Malik said if they upset him – if he got angry – fires would just start up. Kitchen, corner of the living room – telly exploded.

SHABIR. So you agreed to an exorcism?

MUSTAFA. No. I saw the boy, sat with him. We prayed together. Seemed to be doing okay, even ate with him, to encourage him, and he managed to get some food in and some sleep. Then one day I'm sitting on the settee with Malik and his daughter and Kamran gets angry. Starts yelling, kicking off.

SHABIR. Kicking off?

MUSTAFA. Screaming, he was in a rage – his voice wasn't his own, it was...

SHABIR. There are mental conditions that –

MUSTAFA. He grabbed one foot of the settee and lifts it right up – with us three still on it. Three, maybe four feet in the air. Slams it down. His sister goes flying, Malik starts having an asthma attack...

SHABIR *scribbles a note down.*

Mental conditions exist, course they do, voices can change, people self-harm... But no one lights a fire in a room they're not in without so much as a match... no one lifts three people and a settee four foot into the air one-handed cos of some mental disorder.

SHABIR. But with all the chaos and Malik's asthma – the family were already so distressed that...

MUSTAFA. They imagined it? That we all hallucinated together?

SHABIR. I'm not [saying that] –

MUSTAFA. Yes you are. I don't know what it is about the truth when it gets a bit difficult, out of the norm. Passes from me to you and it becomes... a tale. A comic book – bit of entertainment.

SHABIR. I'm trying to understand.

MUSTAFA. So if you don't understand then it's not true? It didn't happen?

SHABIR. This is no time for philosophising, Mustafa. You went into a room with a perfectly healthy seventeen-year-old and when you came out he was dead.

MUSTAFA. Perfectly healthy? Have you been listening to anything I've –

SHABIR. He was alive. He was alive and then he wasn't. You were in there with him. You were the only one in there with him.

MUSTAFA. You're trying to make sense out of it. Cold, British, legal sense. Your face, looks just like the barrister and the jury and the judge. You should go.

SHABIR. Mustafa –

MUSTAFA. It's time for Asr.

SHABIR. See, this is what you do – always – you walk away.

MUSTAFA. I'm not going anywhere. Not for a long time.

SHABIR. And I want to change that. But I just don't see how –

MUSTAFA. You don't have to see, you have to believe.

SHABIR. You pleaded not guilty.

MUSTAFA. I'm in prison because a boy died. I pleaded not guilty because I didn't take his life. But he died, and I can't change that.

MUSTAFA *stands.* SHABIR *begins, reluctantly, to gather his things together. As* MUSTAFA *passes to get to the door,* SHABIR *grabs his hand.*

SHABIR. I've heard – about the things that have been going on with you here. The way the officers talk... can't imagine what the prisoners are saying.

MUSTAFA. Did you tell them you're my brother?

SHABIR. It's not the way to go if you want to get out early – you can't keep –

MUSTAFA. I didn't do those things. Any of them.

SHABIR. Enough! Haven't you had enough? What do you expect me to say to that? You smashed a tray in some guy's face – some young, tough, white criminal's face – in here – and you expect things to go smoothly?

MUSTAFA. He did it to himself.

SHABIR. Oh, come on, if you think selling ghost stories to this lot will make your time easier, you're wrong! You scalded some other guy in the showers.

MUSTAFA. The temperature changed – he was goading me and the water got hotter and hotter and he just stood there. You think I control the water temperature in the prison showers?

SHABIR. Then who, Mustafa – if not you, then who?

MUSTAFA. The djinn –

SHABIR. Oh, God help me…

MUSTAFA. – that left the boy is here.

SHABIR. Listen to yourself –

MUSTAFA. I see it, I hear it. Sometimes in the officers. Sometimes in the prisoners. It does things.

SHABIR. This is childish – this is crazy…

MUSTAFA. It's also true. Believe, don't believe, doesn't make it any less true. The world doesn't disappear if you close your eyes to it, Shabir.

SHABIR. Thanks, Yoda. Any more pearls of wisdom?

MUSTAFA *smiles*.

What could possibly be amusing right now?

MUSTAFA. We watched that together, Yoda, Han Solo, Luke…

SHABIR. Yes.

MUSTAFA. I broke your Millennium Falcon – remember?

…

SHABIR. Malik says he wants to visit. It'll look good – victim's father coming to see you – both here and in court. You should see him.

MUSTAFA *shakes his head*.

MUSTAFA. The *Star Wars Trilogy* at the Odeon in town – all three films back to back. That was a good day.

SHABIR. It was a good day. Not like this.

MUSTAFA. I didn't want you to get mixed up in this. That's why I didn't call.

SHABIR. I'll look over the paperwork tonight.

End of scene.

Scene Eight

The next morning – the weekend shift. MUSTAFA's cell. It is dark, the only light is from the small window. DAN stands outside the cell in the corridor and switches on the lights at the wall. Both corridor and cell are flooded with light.

DAN. Let there be light!

He turns his back to the cell and calls another part of the prison with the phone on the wall. MUSTAFA appears in the empty cell – unnoticed by DAN. He is seated on the bed. His face seems to have healed. MUSTAFA's manner of speech and movement is that of LEN at the end of Scene Three and DAN in Scene Six earlier.

(*On phone.*) Yeah, Dave, it's me, just dodgy leccy like you said – it's working now. Yeah, I know… probably went out last night. Well, if he shared with someone without causing trouble he wouldn't be down this end. Yeah, thanks, mate.

MUSTAFA. I didn't cause any trouble.

DAN (*jumps*). Fucking hell! What you doing back – thought you were with your solicitor?

MUSTAFA. I'm back.

DAN. Yeah, but I was here and –

MUSTAFA. And?

DAN. Heard you were having some trouble with the lights in here. Fuses gone – that's all. Fixed now.

MUSTAFA. That's good of you.

DAN. You ain't scared of the dark?

MUSTAFA. There's no need to be scared, Dan.

DAN. Nah, I ain't saying I am – I'm just saying –

MUSTAFA. How are you?

DAN *is still a little unnerved by* MUSTAFA*'s sudden appearance, but stands his ground.*

DAN. I got better things to do but I'm having to work the weekend. Not too happy about that, Muzz. 'Specially since we're usually okay with one man down, 'cept that you're in here and need checking every hour.

MUSTAFA. I see.

DAN. It's different with the other guys. They talk – bit of banter, chat about this and that, *Junior Apprentice, Corrie –* you know, banter. But with you...

MUSTAFA. Ah... I bore you?

DAN. Yeah, as a matter of fact.

MUSTAFA *laughs.*

How's your face healing up?

DAN *steps closer to take a look at* MUSTAFA*'s face.*

MUSTAFA. Like a peach.

DAN. Shittin' 'ell! ... Looks... Looks like nothing ever happened. What you do, voodoo your bruises away?

MUSTAFA. Not voodoo. But right idea, I guess.

DAN *stares at* MUSTAFA*'s face.*

Something bugging you, Dan?

DAN. You, mate, always... Have to make the trek over, don't I.

MUSTAFA. *'S just a corridor, Len... Well, some of us could do without the extra exercise...*

DAN. What d'you say?

MUSTAFA. *Jeez, can't get the staff as it is... Thanks a lot!... Pleasure's all mine...*

DAN *steps back, disturbed by* MUSTAFA*'s missing bruises and his words.*

DAN *(nervous).* I thought you were in with your new solicitor.

MUSTAFA. No.

DAN. It's good. Asian bloke, I heard, speaks your language and all that.

MUSTAFA. Yeah, cos I can't last a day without a conversation in – (*Exaggerated and anglicised.*) Punjaaaaabi.

DAN (*laughs, uncomfortable*). Punjabi, yeah.

> MUSTAFA *laughs with* DAN, *it's the first time* DAN*'s seen the prisoner laugh and something about it is unsettling.*

You okay?

MUSTAFA. Yeah.

DAN. Well, then maybe you can tell me what's going on – with your face – and who brought you back from the goldfish bowl just now?

MUSTAFA (*stares at* DAN). I don't know what you're talking about.

DAN (*offended*). No, you wouldn't, would ya. Like I say to the other officers, no banter with our magic man. Although I don't get why you don't like being called *magic man*. I mean, if it was racial abuse or something I think I'd get it, but magic man? Could be seen as a compliment, if you were… Paul Daniels?

> MUSTAFA *stares at* DAN.

You hear me? Oi!

> DAN *is unnerved by* MUSTAFA*'s stare.*

Oi! I'm talking to you – don't you know it's rude to stare?

MUSTAFA. Who taught you that, Dan?

> MUSTAFA *leans closer to the bars* (*and* DAN).

Your mummy?

DAN. Piss off!

MUSTAFA. You ought to get that looked at.

DAN. Eh?

MUSTAFA. Might have a bruised rib, maybe fractured.

DAN. What?

MUSTAFA. Does it hurt, Dan?

DAN. Dunno what you're talking about, mate –

MUSTAFA. Your ribs. Right side.

DAN. It… it was an accident –

MUSTAFA. With an iron?

DAN. How… Yeah, I mean I was ironing something and it…

MUSTAFA. Accidentally swung round and caught you in the ribs?

DAN. Fucking hell…

MUSTAFA. Exactly. What's the matter, Dan, don't you want to play?

DAN (*angry*). It was an accident. I don't wanna hear any different, all right?

MUSTAFA. And who do you think I'm going to discuss your domestic set-up with?

DAN. Like you know anything! I swear, you open your mouth to anyone and –

MUSTAFA. And?

DAN. And –

MUSTAFA. And?

DAN *is lost for words.*

You know, I can show you some magic, Dan, if you really want me to. What's it worth?

DAN. What?

MUSTAFA. What's it worth, Dan – my magic?

DAN. It's… I dunno… Just…

MUSTAFA. Just…?

DAN. Shut up! Shut up before I…

MUSTAFA. Ooh, Dan, that's really scary…

DAN. I mean it – you stop this or I'll have to come in there.

MUSTAFA. Ooh yeah, you would, wouldn't you...

MUSTAFA *steps aside, waiting for* DAN *to reach for his keys, unlock the door and step into the cell.* DAN *doesn't move.*

DAN. Lucky for you I gotta finish my rounds.

MUSTAFA. Yes, Danny boy.

DAN. What did you say?

MUSTAFA. *Don't worry, Danny boy, Mummy's gonna look after ya...*

DAN. Mustafa?

MUSTAFA (*laughs heartily*). Oh, we know all about you, don't we, Danny boy! Tell me, what's it like going with a woman twice your age? I mean, is that it – really – you just miss your mum so you decide to live with someone who's the same age?

DAN. I don't know what you're doing, but you better fucking s[top] –

MUSTAFA (*stops laughing*). Stop? It's not that easy to do, though, is it...? See, *once I get started... I just can't help myself...*

DAN. What are you doing?

MUSTAFA (*impersonating* DAN). *Thing is, Pam... we're short-staffed at work so I've been asked to work the weekend. Only just found out, angel...*

DAN. Stop.

MUSTAFA (*impersonating* DAN). *Sweetheart, it's not like I planned it – is it, petal? Guv's got his eye on me already so I couldn't refuse, could I? I booked the day off, honest, but 's just the way it turned out... Angel...?* Danny boy's little angel... But angel wasn't very happy, was she, when Danny boy fucked up and didn't make it to her cousin's birthday bash... Go on, Danny – flash us your chest... let me see what she left for you... Come on, show me what she left you for telling porky pies...

DAN. What the hell are you playing at?

MUSTAFA. Don't like it, do you, Danny boy –

DAN. Stop calling me that! Stop it!

MUSTAFA. – don't like it when the lads get on your back about being a mummy's boy. That's what she called you, isn't it… *Danny boy.*

DAN. Shut it!

MUSTAFA. What's the matter – I thought you liked magic? Come on, Dan, what do you miss the most, eh? When she used to sing you to sleep after your bad dreams…? Now, what was that song…?

DAN *is scared.*

No singing now though, is there, Danny boy? But Pam does it for you in other ways… (*Impersonating* DAN *in distress.*) *Don't… don't do it, angel… (Tears.) Pam, please don't – you promised, remember! Don't – don't hurt me!*

DAN *is near tears of rage as much as fear.*

DAN. Fucking freak!

MUSTAFA. Easy, Danny boy, easy. I know it's tough for you –

DAN. You don't know jack shit!

MUSTAFA. Oh, but I do… that's the thing about me… I know things.

DAN *struggles with his keys and tries to back out of the corridor, he stumbles and falls.*

Oh yeah! I remember now. (*Sings.*) Save… all… your… kisses for me, save all your kisses for me. Bye-bye, baby, bye-bye… don't cry, honey, don't cry…

DAN *cries and screams on the floor.*

DAN. Stop! Stop! Stop!

MUSTAFA *laughs, and in a moment the cell is empty once again. The lights fade until all we see is the silhouette of* DAN, *on the floor against the wall. We hear only* DAN's *sobs and then he is quiet. Lights up a moment later.* LEN *enters.*

LEN. Well, looks like they fixed the lights. Dan, what you doing down there? Dan? You all right? Dan?

DAN *stares at* LEN *in a dazed shock. He stands, slowly, warily, his watery eyes fixed on what is now an empty cell.*

Dan, what happened – you feeling okay?

DAN. What the fuck do you think? How…

LEN. Look at me, you okay? What happened?

DAN. He… Where is he?

LEN. Who?

DAN. Where is he?!

LEN. What, Mustafa? He's in with his solicitor – think they're going to be a while – guy was late, just got here. Chris is covering the goldfish bowl – so I came to check the lights. Dave said the fuse'd blown.

DAN *grabs his keys and tries to unlock the cell door but his hands are shaking violently.*

DAN. Nah, nah – can't be. He's… Where'd he go?

LEN. Maybe we should talk somewhere else, come on –

DAN (*shouts*). Where did you just take him?

LEN. He's in the goldfish bowl waiting for his solicitor – what happened?

DAN. But that… It…

LEN. Dan?

DAN. He was just…

LEN. Come on, son, let's –

DAN. I am not your son! I'm… I'm… You told him. You did –

LEN. I don't know what's going on, but we are not doing this here. Now move it.

LEN *grabs* DAN *and forces him out of the corridor.*

I think you need some fresh air.

Lights down.

End of scene.

Scene Nine

Same day, continuous. The goldfish bowl. MUSTAFA is seated, waiting for SHABIR. He has his book with him and is reading it silently, a few loose leaves spread out on the table. SHABIR enters. He hasn't slept and looks tired, wearing clothes from the day before. All he has with him is a paper file with pages haphazardly stuffed in it. He stays standing, unable to keep still. He is distressed and trying not to show it.

MUSTAFA. Assalamu alaikum.

> SHABIR *avoids* MUSTAFA*'s gaze and paces.*

> Shabir?

> …

SHABIR. There's a new guy at the firm. He's good, very good. He'll take your case – no expense, I'll take care of that, I can do that. I'll pass on your files, get him up to date.

> …

MUSTAFA. Right. Has something happened? Shabir, if something happened then you need to tell me.

> …

SHABIR. I… I looked at the files… been avoiding them since I got them but then last night… I can't, Mustafa, I…

MUSTAFA. What happened – did something happen last night?

SHABIR. The medical reports. On the boy… It's… I… (*Sifts through file in his hands bewildered.*) Broken ribs, broken nose, dislocated arm… punctured lung. Fractured skull… Cuts, bruising all over his body…

> *Disturbed, he puts the file and papers on the table.*

> The photos… What you… What happened… I just can't.

MUSTAFA. Oh. Right. I understand.

SHABIR. No you don't! You don't understand, Mustafa! Look at this – read it! It's… it's… I can't believe you'd…

MUSTAFA. Say it.

SHABIR.…

MUSTAFA. Go on. Say it. If you believe that I… you have to say it. Please!

…

SHABIR. Two whiskies before I came. And even then I wasn't numb enough. Kept thinking to myself, any more than two and you'll smell it on me – you always did. You were right, about the drink. And Mary and I were together before we married – and yes, it was a civil ceremony because she didn't convert.

MUSTAFA. Shabir?

SHABIR. I didn't need her to. Or maybe I didn't even want her to. I walked the corridors of Ashcroft Bailey and Monk for years – listened to their bastard comments… racist, bigoted comments… and they come out with them at the most… unpredictable times… Like it's in their blood or something. Like they know how much I need to get to where they have in life and somehow they just don't want me to make it. The cream of the crop, know which fork to use for the salad and what to wear to the opera, and which wine goes best with fucking foie gras. All that education… all that time spent learning and not one of them even knows the basics of how to treat another human being. I thought, fine, if this is the way it's going to be, fine. See, I'm not like you, I don't mind changing to fit in – whatever it takes for the end goal… And my end goal is here, Mustafa – in the world – not after, not in the unknown. I grafted and brown-nosed like the best of them – better in fact. Told them I was alone in England, that I didn't have any family over here!

MUSTAFA. Shabir…

SHABIR. And I didn't feel bad – lying. Every fucking Christmas raising a glass of bubbly to the company – because God knows if they caught you with an OJ they knew you just weren't man enough… I didn't see you. I couldn't, could I? 'Specially after 9/11, you with your Bin Laden outfits and beard and… But me, I kept my mind focused on the prize. Got to a point where I liked not seeing you – it was easier that way. Just easier… I changed my surname so no one could ever make the link. I knew you'd never come to the office, so… I didn't think you'd ever know.

MUSTAFA. It's all right –

SHABIR. No! No, it's not all right!… Was thinking about it all last night… We're all out to have it easy because we like it that way. But not you. Easier to drink and forget, it's easier to love sport more than God, it's easier to get a new wife when you're bored of the one you've got – it's bloody easier not to see family if they're a pain in the arse or, God forbid, an embarrassment! But in all that time – the whole time – I knew you'd be praying for me. … When I was drunk out of my tree, you know, I'd laugh about it; my naive brother who hasn't really seen the world will be praying for my soul and missing out on the party… But sometimes – most times – I'd be… grateful… just so fucking grateful that in amongst all the… shit… there was one… pure thing. You. But this… it's just…

…

(*Wipes his face and tears*.) But, this new guy, he can do something, I'm confident he can [help] –

MUSTAFA. What happened, Shabir?

SHABIR. Huh?

MUSTAFA. I went in that room with the boy when he was alive, just like you said, and then he came out like this – (*Picks up a fist full of the medical papers*.) So what happened in the room?

SHABIR.…

MUSTAFA. What are you thinking? I want to hear it!

SHABIR. You were in there with him.

MUSTAFA. Yes, I was – I haven't denied that fact from that day to this! What do you think I did? Tell me!

SHABIR *sits, unable to speak, aware of the officer outside*.

I don't care what they think out there, I don't care what the law thinks – what the prisoners or officers in here think. But I do care what… [you think].

SHABIR. You did this. You! His family's outside, his parents – who love him – are right outside the door. You're in there with him and he comes out like this and you want me and the rest of the world to think it was some… entity?

MUSTAFA. Djinn are mentioned throughout the Qur'ān.

SHABIR. I give up.

MUSTAFA. Beings created from fire like we are from earth.

SHABIR. For God's sake, M[ustafa] –

MUSTAFA. Yes! God. For God's sake! I'm reminding you of what you knew once. What you bel[ieved] –

SHABIR. Don't make me say it! Don't you dare make me say what you did! This is your doing – spit it out!

Long pause.

MUSTAFA. I kept going to him, Kamran, didn't want him to feel alone.

SHABIR. Maybe I can't do this.

MUSTAFA (*determined*). I saw a few more episodes when he was taken over by it. Then he got sick. Sicker. Weaker.

SHABIR. I can't be your confessor…

MUSTAFA. We were sat reciting Qur'ān and one day he just wouldn't stop crying… Malik told me later that Kamran attacked his sister. They were home alone while Malik and his wife went to see this peer in Bradford and he attacked her. It attacked her. That's when he insisted they lock him in his room. And that was it. He didn't want it any more. He needed me to help and I couldn't refuse him.

SHABIR. You mean you wouldn't.

MUSTAFA. No.

SHABIR. They could have asked someone else – someone qualified – there's a dozen peers out there, they're selling their services on telly, for Christ's sake!

MUSTAFA. And you think they would have helped him – some money-grabbing televangelists?

SHABIR. And you did help him? Huh? (*Holds a photo up to* MUSTAFA.) This is help?

It's the first time MUSTAFA *has looked at an image of Kamran since the trial.*

Answer me.

SHABIR *grabs* MUSTAFA's *hand.*

Answer me! How did the boy get like this?

MUSTAFA. Because I was scared, okay! I was terrified, Shabir! And somehow, somewhere, I missed something – I must have... Do you hear me? The boy is like that because I messed it up – because I was scared!

...

I told him the risks – I prayed hard, studied, spoke to people, and even then I went back to him and told him I've not done this before – I want to help but I don't think this is the way! But he was so desperate. He was clear that he didn't want to live with that thing inside him. He didn't want to see his parents and sister disintegrate in front of him – with him – because of this... thing. And, you're right, I couldn't say no. But I was... scared...

End of scene.

Scene Ten

Same day, continuous. Exterior. Prison grounds. DAN *is smoking.* LEN *approaches with two coffees.*

LEN. How you doing?

LEN *holds out a drink for* DAN.

DAN. How long did you say he was with his solicitor?

LEN. I got someone to cover – no one needs to know about this.

DAN. Thanks, Len – I need this job – you know if I went home without –

LEN. But I'm not going to put you, us or the inmates at risk...

DAN. What do you mean?

LEN. I need to know what happened – and no shaky shit, just give it to me straight.

LEN *puts one cup on the ground as* DAN *doesn't want it.*

DAN. I already told ya –

LEN. So you're sticking to the story –

DAN. It ain't a story!

LEN. That the inmate was in his cell when I was stood outside the goldfish bowl watching him wait for his solicitor – that's what you're telling me?

DAN (*unsure*). Yeah…

LEN. And you want me to keep this quiet?

DAN. I don't… I don't know what I want…

LEN. You've been drinking.

DAN. No, I –

LEN (*angry*). I smelt it on your breath, Dan. I know when you've crawled in after a rough night, but pull a stunt like this and you'll end up fired for good! No wonder you're hallucinating like –

DAN. Don't, Len – not you!

LEN. You been taking anything else? Eh? Look at me.

DAN. I had a drink cos me and Pam had a fight, okay! A stupid fucking fight and it was one drink! You really fucking think I'd make this up off the top of my head? A whole conversation with magic Mustafa the f… freak!

LEN. If we continue this conversation you are going to have to address the prisoner with his –

DAN. Oh, get off your high horse!

LEN. It's calling him magic man and magic Mustafa that's got you all worked up!

DAN *throws his cigarette down and lights another.*

So what, you think you saw him in his cell and –

DAN. I did see him.

LEN. Okay, okay, so he was in his cell and what?

DAN. What's his face like?

LEN. What?

DAN. When you saw him just now – is it still bruised up?

LEN. Course it's still bruised.

DAN. But did you see him up close?

LEN. What, do you think he's been overdoing the Olay Regenerist, Dan?

DAN. Don't take the piss –

LEN. Oh, you think I'm amused, do you? You think any part of this is amusing? I'm this close to retirement – you need this job cos it's a miracle you got it in the first place – and you think I'm pissing in the wind?

DAN. Okay – well, I'll be honest if you are.

LEN. I'm not in the mood for games.

DAN. That time, after your one-to-one with him, when you were feeling faint.

LEN. What?

DAN. When you talked to him about Tony and the dinner tray.

LEN. Yeah?

DAN. What happened?

LEN. What do you mean, what happened, we had a meeting and then it was over.

DAN. Who knocked the chair over?

LEN. What chair – what the hell are you –

DAN *pulls a handkerchief out of his pocket.*

What's that?

DAN. Your hanky. The only bloke I know who carries a fucking hanky.

LEN *is silent.*

Found it in his cell. Bloodstained.

LEN (*confused*). Well, he must have started bleeding and so I handed him my –

DAN. Just started bleeding out of the blue, did he?

LEN. Yeah.

DAN. Just like that.

LEN. Yes.

> LEN *throws his cup on the ground.*

DAN. You were acting strange that whole morning after that meeting – went home sick – not like you.

LEN. I wasn't feeling too great, that's all.

DAN. Like me, Len, you weren't feeling too great cos something happened and –

LEN. I don't know what happened – I don't know if anything *did* happen…

DAN. He was bleeding, Len – he was bleeding and the chair was on the floor!

LEN. Nothing happened – I… I asked him, okay – I told him if I misbehaved, if he wanted another PO, I'd have a word.

DAN. And?

LEN. Nothing happened.

DAN. Mo says he's got a genie.

LEN. Oh, for fuck's [sake] –

DAN. He got a genie out of that young lad he killed and he's kept it to protect himself!

LEN. Mo is a goon who's been in and out of here since he was sixteen – he doesn't know jack.

DAN. Says he can use it any time he wants…

> LEN *grabs* DAN *by his jacket and pushes him up against the wall.* DAN *groans in pain from his injury.*

LEN. We don't need this, Dan. You hear me? We just need to pray his solicitor gets him his appeal –

DAN *(in pain)*. Thought you never prayed.

> *He looks furious enough to strike* DAN, *but lets him go.* DAN *folds over in pain, holding his right side.*

LEN. Thirty years I spent in here – never broke the golden rule – never. We don't need to know what they're in here for, Dan. Magic, violence, rape, murder, whatever the hell it is, we're best off steering clear of that information. Pain in the arse, kids like you, it's like this is school or something, not a job! Walk around trying to be pals with the cons or bitching about them or finding out what they're in for. We stay calm, they stay calm – simple as. I knew the minute you lot starting winding him up cos of the magic shit that this was gonna go pear-shaped. We are not going in for this mumbo-jumbo nonsense, do you hear me?

LEN *clocks* DAN*'s pain.*

What – you hurt? Dan, are you –

He tries to hold DAN *to steady him, but* DAN *pushes him away. They both stand leaning against the wall for a moment.*

Has he hurt you? Did he hurt you?

DAN. No. Leave off.

LEN. Want me to take a look?

DAN (*moving away*). No – it's fine, 's just…

LEN *tries again to get near* DAN, *but he keeps moving away.*

LEN. Have you had it looked at?

DAN. No need, get lost!

LEN. Dan, it could be serious.

DAN. I said get lost, you woofter – what d'you think this is, fucking kiss-chase?!

LEN. Well, if it's nothing, just let me check you over.

DAN. No! (*Stops and covers his ears.*) No. No. No. No. No!

LEN *finally gets near* DAN, *he wants to comfort him, but seeing his state he doesn't touch him.* DAN *sits on the ground, opens his eyes and uncovers his ears.* LEN *sits beside him.*

LEN. Not again, Dan –

DAN. No – no, not again, it was an accident, just leave it, will ya!

LEN. What'd she do this time – accidentally slam you with a sledgehammer?

DAN. Who you been talking to?

LEN. Oh, give me a break –

DAN. It was him, wasn't it?

LEN. Why are you fixated on him, Dan – I'm talking about that Pamela!

DAN. It's just Pam, all right, Pam – just PAM!

LEN. Sorry.

DAN. She… she was upset. It was my fault cos she was expecting us to… to…

LEN. You don't actually believe that, do you, son?

DAN. Don't know what I believe, Len.

…

LEN *stands and brushes himself off.*

LEN. Right. Break's over. Maybe you should go home, rest up – can't stay here in that state. I'll tell 'em you got a gyppy tummy or something.

DAN. He said things, Len. Things he couldn't have known…

LEN. People go to great lengths to mess you up – been watching this documentary on fraud and identity theft. Unbelievable. Go through your rubbish – take your receipts –

DAN. So he broke out, got my address, went to my house and went through my bins, did he?

LEN. I'm just saying –

DAN. He knew things, Len. It ain't no magic trick. He knew.

DAN *lights up another cigarette,* LEN *looks worried.*

Lights fade.

End of scene.

Scene Eleven

Same day, continuous. The goldfish bowl. MUSTAFA *is sitting on the floor with his head in his hands.* SHABIR *enters with two plastic cups of water. He sits, placing one cup on the end of the table for his brother.*

SHABIR. I bought us some more time. Water?

MUSTAFA. No, Jazakallah Khair.

SHABIR. You should drink something at [least] –

MUSTAFA. I'm fasting.

> SHABIR *downs his water – and then the cup he brought for* MUSTAFA.

> You should never have come. Malik should never have told you.

SHABIR. But he did, and now I'm here. He's been sending visitation requests since you came in.

MUSTAFA. I know.

SHABIR. You've refused every one.

> …

> There must be a reason.

MUSTAFA (*soft*). Malik loved his boy. I can't look him in the face and see his sadness for me… not when he's lost his son. It's right… I was weak because I was scared … I was reciting – sweat pouring down my face – into my eyes – while Kamran was screaming and being… bounced around the room and off the walls like a ball. If I'd stopped in the middle – if I'd left the recitations unfinished, it would have unleashed the damn thing on the whole house. And the whole time, in the moments when Kamran was… Kamran… he kept begging me to carry on, not to stop – to rid him of it – no matter what. No – matter – what.

> …

> When I think what he went through… Everywhere I go, everyone who looks at me, they all see my crime but they weren't there, they don't know.

SHABIR. But you were – and you do.

MUSTAFA. You want me to prove how I wrenched a djinn from the body of that boy when you don't even believe they exist. How am I supposed to do that, huh? I saw fires sprout out of nowhere when he got angry, I saw him say the impossible, do the impossible with the body of a broken seventeen-year-old and no one believes it. In court, they had an expert say it was impossible for me to have inflicted such violence and not have a drop of the boy's blood or sweat on me – not a drop! And still they all looked at *me* funny – like they were trying to work out how the hell I managed to do that to the boy and then clean myself up before the family came in! Why? Because the other option was too difficult. Even when the facts pointed towards it, it's easier to believe the mad-Mullah theory. You, them, all looking at me like I'm a monster!

...

SHABIR *is finding this difficult to hear. We see from his physical responses to* MUSTAFA*'s words that he is disturbed by the notion of the djinn and his brother's belief in it.*

These... things... they rip you up from the inside, because that's where they are. His sister, that's where it would have gone next – it's told me as much. So I just closed my eyes and crouched in a corner and recited and recited till it all stopped – I wanted it to stop, just like Kamran. Don't you get it? He gave his life – and his family? They'll never be the same again. But that djinn is here and I am not going to risk putting it in the same room as Malik. Never.

...

SHABIR. It's here?

MUSTAFA. Yes.

SHABIR. What, right now? Why doesn't it show itself?

MUSTAFA *shakes his head.*

What?

MUSTAFA. It had the boy.

SHABIR. Yes.

MUSTAFA. And I took him from it.

SHABIR. Yes.

MUSTAFA. So who do you think gets me in trouble, eh? Turns warm water scalding in the showers, trips some meathead up during exercise? It wouldn't show itself now, because I want it to – need it to.

SHABIR. Of course.

MUSTAFA. They're keeping me in isolation, though, one good thing. Obviously what happened with Kamran almost worked, almost. It's here, it messes about in the prison but it can't leave. Like it's bound to me in some way... I've been trying to keep it in control. Been reading, trying to find a way –

SHABIR. Right, so everything it does, it does behind closed doors? Where there are no witnesses?

MUSTAFA. People who don't know what they're seeing don't know what they are witnessing.

SHABIR. And the only one who knows is you?

MUSTAFA. What are you trying to say?

SHABIR. I'm stating the facts.

MUSTAFA. You don't need an excuse not to be here, Shabir. No appeal. You're right. This is where I should be. I accept that.

SHABIR. That's not what I think.

MUSTAFA. Yes it is.

SHABIR. So just because I can't say it – just because I can't get on board with this whole... you're going to accept fourteen years?

MUSTAFA. Less if I behave, you said.

SHABIR. And will you, behave?

MUSTAFA. I'm working on it.

SHABIR *picks up* MUSTAFA*'s book from the table. He flicks through it.*

SHABIR. And this is your 'work'?

MUSTAFA. Some of it, yes. Me and a brother studied together –

SHABIR. Brother?

MUSTAFA. Yes.

SHABIR. Oh, you mean a 'brother'.

MUSTAFA. We studied together when I was abroad – we're still in [touch] –

SHABIR. Not like me, then, you mean a brother that counts, right, in the afterlife?

MUSTAFA. Don't do this.

SHABIR. Do what, Mustafa? Help?

MUSTAFA. You can't help me – you don't even believe me!

SHABIR. I'm trying to make you see how this is – how ridiculous it sounds!

MUSTAFA. Don't say that.

SHABIR. Why?

MUSTAFA. Is that why you're upset? Not that I'm accused of doing this to a boy but because I did it out of faith? It isn't easy for me – the way you live… but I've never –

SHABIR. Oh, please, don't even try. You've never judged me, is that what you're about to say?

MUSTAFA. I disagree with so many things you do and say and believe and don't believe – but it's never stopped me loving you. I have never judged you.

SHABIR. Like hell you haven't… You and your bloody brothers!

SHABIR *flings the notebook across the room.*

MUSTAFA. Shabir – no!

MUSTAFA *scrambles across the floor, upset, trying to gather the loose pages and the book as quickly as possible – not wanting his gathered words from the Qur'ān to be on the floor.* SHABIR *watches his brother, torn between helping and getting out. He picks up a page or two near him and hands them to* MUSTAFA.

SHABIR. I'm sorry.

MUSTAFA *scans the room for any lost papers.*

If you continue like this, there isn't a judge in the world that would change the sentence.

MUSTAFA. I don't want that – I need to end this.

SHABIR. Listen to me!

MUSTAFA. I've heard enough. Do you believe me?

...

SHABIR. I knew... Do you understand?

...

I knew before Malik ever came to see me...

...

I stayed away because –

MUSTAFA. You don't need to explain.

SHABIR. Because I knew this is what you'd ask of me.

MUSTAFA. Do you believe me?

SHABIR. And I can't give it.

MUSTAFA. Shabir, do you believe me?

SHABIR *gathers the papers on the table – not caring how he does it.*

(*Desperate.*) Shabir?

SHABIR *takes his things and leaves the room.* MUSTAFA *watches after him.*

End of scene.

Scene Twelve

MUSTAFA *washes for prayer. The movement is routine, something he's done all his adult years, at least five times a day. It is precise, and soothing.*

He stands at his prayer mat. He prays Salaat and, as he does – as he stands, hands folded, sits, hands on knees, and prostrates himself, his forehead on the mat – the light in the cell changes indicating the passage of time.

Afterwards he makes dua, sitting with his hands out in front of him, his prayer is silent but his face is desperate, emotional. Emotion turns to tears and he submits once again, resting his forehead on the mat. He remains in that position, vulnerable, and alone.

The light continues to change as days pass. MUSTAFA sits up, wipes his face. He stands at the prayer mat again, this time determined.

End of scene.

Scene Thirteen

A small exercise yard penned in by high walls of the prison buildings. A week has passed since we last saw MUSTAFA with SHABIR. It is nearing sunset. MUSTAFA walks in circles, slowly, he's deep in thought. His bruises have healed a little more since we last saw him. LEN stands leaning against a wall, watching.

MUSTAFA. Tell me something about yourself, Len.

LEN. I reckon I can run faster than you.

MUSTAFA (*manages a smile*). Something I don't know already.

LEN. Rule goes both ways – you don't get the skinny on the prisoners, and they don't get the skinny on you.

MUSTAFA. You a stickler for the rules?

LEN. Just neater that way.

MUSTAFA. You like things neat?

LEN. Can't say I mind. Wife's into keeping everything in its place – I go along with it.

MUSTAFA. Fair enough. Kids?

...

LEN. How come you're so chatty, fresh air gone to your head?

MUSTAFA. Nice to be out.

LEN. You've refused for how many days now?

MUSTAFA. Been distracted.

LEN. By what, pool practice?

MUSTAFA. No, unfortunately not pool.

LEN. Your brother hasn't come recently.

MUSTAFA. No.

LEN. And your appeal?

MUSTAFA. I thought you weren't into details.

LEN. You said he's your brother – seeing as you don't speak to anyone else, I thought…

MUSTAFA.…

LEN. The guv called me in. They're putting you back on the wing.

MUSTAFA *stops walking.*

I told you it wouldn't be for ever.

MUSTAFA. When?

LEN. We got officers on leave – Dan's off sick – we can't cover the old wing for just one prisoner.

MUSTAFA. When?

LEN. A day, maybe two…

After a moment of concern, MUSTAFA *laughs.*

You okay?

MUSTAFA. It had to be some time – (*Looking at the sky.*) I guess now's better than any.

LEN. Things have calmed down, I'm sure you won't have any trouble.

MUSTAFA. I can't be around other prisoners, Len, I can't share a cell, not yet.

LEN. It'll be all right, son, you'll be okay.

MUSTAFA *sits.*

Not long to go, you want to spend it sitting?

LEN *looks around and then approaches the prisoner. He pulls a chocolate bar out of his pocket.*

Here.

MUSTAFA *looks at it.*

Go on, take it. Sorry, it's the best I can do – but you look like you need it.

MUSTAFA *takes it.*

MUSTAFA. Thanks. Used to be my favourite.

LEN. What, you don't eat chocolate any more?

MUSTAFA. Guess not. (*Eating.*) You're a good man, Len.

LEN. There aren't any good men or bad men, Mustafa – only good and bad choices. I know it might be simple, but it's what I believe.

MUSTAFA. And what if a good choice results in something bad – when you didn't intend it to?

LEN. I dunno, I guess you've gotta learn from it. If you can't do that then it's all for nothing.

Both men enjoy the outside air for a moment.

MUSTAFA. Len, I'm going to need a favour.

…

LEN. I'm listening.

MUSTAFA. I need to be in the cell for at least two more days – can you make sure it's two?

LEN. Why?

MUSTAFA. There's something I need to do and I need a couple more days.

LEN. Something I want to know about?

MUSTAFA. No. I just need to know I got the cell for a couple more days, it'll probably only take one, but just in case.

LEN. Sounds intriguing.

MUSTAFA. Do you know who's on nights?

LEN. Why, you planning an escape?

MUSTAFA *laughs*.

Most likely me, or Chris.

MUSTAFA. Be good if it was you.

LEN. Okay, now I am intrigued.

MUSTAFA. Len, I need you not to look in on me.

LEN. What?

MUSTAFA. I just need you not to look in on the old block until morning.

LEN. No can do, Mustafa – thems the rules.

MUSTAFA. Len –

LEN. Dan said he saw you in your cell last week. He said he saw you and talked to you.

MUSTAFA....

LEN. He said he was talking to you in your cell when I was with you waiting for your solicitor to turn up. In the goldfish bowl.

MUSTAFA. He okay?

LEN. Dunno. Coming back tomorrow, find out soon enough.

...

MUSTAFA. Man can't be in two places at one time.

LEN. That's what I said.

The men look at one another for a moment.

I can make sure you get two nights, and I'll make sure I'm working them. But I will be looking in every hour on the hour. Thems the rules, Mustafa.

End of scene.

Scene Fourteen

The next day. DAN *stands outside the prison smoking a cigarette. He has a bandage on one hand.* LEN *walks over to him.*

LEN. Thought I'd find you here. Chris said you were back.

DAN. Yeah, I'm back.

LEN. If you need some more time...

DAN. You didn't tell anyone?

LEN. Not a word.

DAN. Good. I'm good.

> *He puts out a cigarette and lights another. The bandage on his hand shows a spot of blood.* LEN *sees this.*

LEN. Dan?

DAN. Yeah.

LEN. Everything okay?

DAN (*inhales*). Yeah.

LEN. What happened to your hand?

> ...

DAN. I finally did it, Len.

LEN. What?

DAN. Been thinking, Len, all last week while I was off. Then yesterday, I just... it was time.

LEN. Dan...?

DAN. Didn't tell her I was off sick. I just got dressed every day last week, made like I was coming to work.

LEN. Where did you go?

DAN. Anywhere, Len. Just didn't want to be there. Yesterday I went to the shopping centre – big one in town. Saw loads of people buying things, eating things, doing things... Working day an' all and I'm thinking, where do they get the time?

LEN. That'll be the recession, son – they're all out of work.

DAN. Nah, nah, Len, they're living, that's what. That was it then. I went home.

LEN (*increasingly concerned as the blood spot spreads on* DAN*'s bandaged hand*). Dan...

DAN. Saw her, sitting by the telly watching *Loose Women* with a Terry's Chocolate Orange.

LEN. Pam?

DAN. Yeah. (*Laughs.*) That Pamela. She jumped out of her skin – not ready for me, was she, not my usual time for coming home. Jumped out her skin so much she gave herself a fucking fag burn! (*Laughs hard.*) Can you believe it, Len, she gave herself one!

LEN. How did you hurt your hand?

DAN. She hit the roof. How come I was home early, how come I didn't call – she needs her time, see, time to herself. I told her I'm not taking it any more, all the shit. Told her I'm not giving her my wages any more, and she can pay for her own fucking fags! Can't believe it, Len, it just spewed out of me – dunno where it came from, but it felt... great...

LEN. What she say?

DAN. Nothing. She threw her ashtray at me head.

He feels a lump on his head.

That was it then, I lunged for her, smacked her in the lip and...

LEN. Dan?

DAN *cries.*

Dan, is she okay?

DAN *takes a moment to recover.*

DAN. My mum used to say a true man would never hit a woman.

LEN. What happened?

DAN. Missed, didn't I. Sod's frickin' Law I end up missing her and I go flying straight through the patio door – right hook first. Least I caught her lip.

DAN *looks at his damaged hand*.

LEN. And that's it?

DAN. Yeah, think so, out like a light, wasn't I. Came to about fifteen, twenty minutes later and she was packing her bags, ranting about how she didn't owe me anything and if I want to go it alone then she can find somewhere else.

LEN. So she's...?

DAN. Gone. To Barbara's, probably.

Beat.

LEN. You didn't stop her?

DAN. No, Len, not this time. I watched her pack every bastard thing I ever bought her, and leave.

LEN (*tentative*). Well, good on you, son. I'm sure it's for the best.

DAN. Yeah. She's gone. Her and her fucking clutter. History. My mum hated clutter. Pam loved the stuff.

The two men stand for a moment as DAN *smokes and* LEN *takes in the news.*

Len.

LEN. Yeah?

DAN. How are things with you and the missus?

LEN. Good, good. Why?

DAN. 'S just... All right if I come home with you tonight? Don't fancy being there, you know, by myself.

LEN. Sure, I'll ring home, let her know.

DAN. Thanks. You're a real mate. (*Beat.*) Bitch took the leccy blanket, didn't she, plays havoc with my back if I ain't warm. You got a leccy blanket at home?

DAN *cries.* LEN *holds him.*

End of scene.

Scene Fifteen

Same day. Evening. MUSTAFA's cell. MUSTAFA is sitting on his bed with his tasbih. He looks weak and tired and has his blanket around him. The bruises on his face have healed some more in the week that has passed. We hear DAN.

DAN (*off*). Mustafa... Mustafa, I'm coming in...

DAN enters the corridor carefully, one step at a time.

Mustafa?

MUSTAFA. Yes.

DAN. Is that you?

MUSTAFA. Dan?

DAN. Is it you?

MUSTAFA. Yes. What are you doing?

We see DAN holding out a photocopy of some Islamic calligraphy. He holds it out like it's a crucifix pointed at a vampire. It's upside down.

DAN. How do I know?

MUSTAFA. What's that?

DAN. It's, er – I got it from the quiet room – photocopied it. Mo said it's a prayer for protection.

MUSTAFA. It's upside down.

DAN. Oh... sorry.

MUSTAFA. Take it you haven't been learning Arabic while you've been off?

DAN. No, no I ain't.

MUSTAFA sees DAN's eyes are red and tired and he has a bandage on one hand.

MUSTAFA. You feeling better?

DAN. Yeah, nah...

DAN drags a chair over to the cell bars. He sits.

Both men are silent for a moment.

Been thinking… and thinking and thinking, see. Whichever way you cut it, I saw what I saw.

…

You… told me things. You… He… Don't fucking know what to call it.

…

Thing is, you said things to me… things no one could have known. 'Cept it wasn't you, was it? I been reading up on it a bit – Googled 'em, you know, djinn, get my head straight. It knew things… It said things – personal things that were between me and Pam… me and my mum…

MUSTAFA. You cared a lot for your mum.

DAN. Yeah – took a lot of stick for it an' all, mind. It was right, though, everything it said – it was right.

MUSTAFA. You're going to be okay.

DAN. You reckon?

MUSTAFA. Yeah.

DAN. Don't s'pose you could knock me up a potion or something?

MUSTAFA. Don't think you need one.

…

I know what they say about you, Dan, but I think you're okay.

DAN. What do they say?

MUSTAFA. You know.

DAN. And what do you think?

MUSTAFA. That's not for me to [say] –

DAN. I wanna know.

MUSTAFA. What she's done to you is a crime.

DAN. Like what you did to that boy?

…

MUSTAFA. This isn't about me.

DAN. 'Cept you didn't, did ya... Just like you said, it wasn't you did those things, with Tony or all them other times. So why ain't you telling anyone? Why ain't you doing something about it?

...

MUSTAFA. What happened to your hand?

DAN. Nothing... 'S just...

MUSTAFA. An accident?

DAN. Yeah, yeah, it really was, as a matter of fact.

MUSTAFA. You're going to be all right.

DAN. And you?

Both men are silent for a moment.

Keep thinking... about that kid. How his folks must have felt watching an ambulance wheel his body away. Did you know he was gonna die?

MUSTAFA. I knew it was possible. We both did.

Lights fade.

End of scene.

Scene Sixteen

Same day. Night. MUSTAFA's cell. It is dark in the cell. The only light is from the corridor. MUSTAFA is sitting in his hisar. LEN enters the corridor and walks up to the cell.

LEN. Mustafa?

MUSTAFA's eyes are closed and he doesn't respond.

Mustafa?

He bangs lightly on the cell bars. MUSTAFA's eyes remain closed as he converses.

MUSTAFA. Didn't think you were working tonight.

LEN. You should be in bed, son, it's gone one a.m.

MUSTAFA. I told you, Len, got things to do, can't sleep.

LEN. Dan came back today, feeling a bit brighter.

MUSTAFA. Yeah.

LEN. Said he came to see you?

MUSTAFA. Yes, he's doing really well, isn't he?

LEN (*with difficulty*). Yeah, yeah. Good.

MUSTAFA. Very.

LEN. He told me, you know, day after it happened. He said it wasn't you – incident in the dining hall, with Tony. Said Tony did it to himself.

MUSTAFA *is silent*.

I didn't believe him before but… now… I know it wasn't you.

MUSTAFA. Sorry, Len…

LEN. Nah, don't worry about it. I should be sorry, son.

MUSTAFA. No. I'm sorry because it was me.

LEN. What?

MUSTAFA. I've been denying it, but the dinner tray, it was me.

LEN. No, son, Dan told me.

MUSTAFA. Thing is, I never liked Tony.

LEN. No. Dan was there and he said you were nowhere near –

MUSTAFA. Allah's blessed me with certain powers, Len. I didn't have to use my body. Just my mind…

The lights begin to flicker.

LEN (*firm*). It wasn't you.

MUSTAFA. Yes it was. And the prisoner in the showers that time? It *was* me.

LEN. No.

MUSTAFA. Yes.

LEN. No –

MUSTAFA. I just have to pray, to concentrate and I can bend the rules of physics...

LEN. No! No you can't, Mustafa! Do you want to know how I know that?

The lights flicker and suddenly LEN *disappears from outside the cell and* DAN *stands right in front of* MUSTAFA, *his boots on the edge of the hisar.* MUSTAFA *opens his eyes.*

DAN. Because it was me...

DAN *laughs.* MUSTAFA *does not flinch.*

MUSTAFA. I've been waiting for you.

DAN. Yeah? I been here all along, Muzz. Been bored an' all, mate – no fun – but now we're moving back among the locals –

MUSTAFA. We?

DAN. Where you go, I go, remember?

MUSTAFA. You've got nowhere to go. Just you and me and this cell.

MUSTAFA *closes his eyes again and starts to recite.*

DAN. What you doing, Muzz, eh? That mumbo-jumbo didn't work last time, you think it's gonna work now?

MUSTAFA *keeps reciting.*

Oi! (*Jumps up onto the bed and shouts down at* MUSTAFA.) Oi!

MUSTAFA *doesn't break his concentration. Slowly we hear the crackling of flames. A fire starts in the far corner of the cell. There is no smoke, but we hear the crackling and see the light from the flames thrown across the cell, growing.*

See, see what I can do, Mustafa! See my power!

LEN *enters the corridor outside. He's shocked by what he sees. He grabs a fire extinguisher from across the corridor.*

LEN. Dan – what you doing in there? Mustafa? Fire!

LEN *grabs his keys fumbling for the right one, with the fire extinguisher under one arm.*

DAN. Come on, Len, come in here and save us!

LEN. Fire! Dan, what are you doing?

MUSTAFA. Len, that is not Dan – it's not Dan. Don't come in here. Don't come in here, whatever you see.

LEN *continues to fumble with the keys.*

LEN. Come on, come on!

MUSTAFA. Listen to me, Len, you need to get out of here, now.

DAN. Don't listen to him, Len, he made me come in here, magic Mustafa – he made me!

DAN *jumps off the bed and into the fire. A moment later* SHABIR *walks out from where* DAN *went.* LEN *drops the extinguisher.* SHABIR *looks smart, in a crisp suit dressed for court.*

LEN. Mustafa? Dan? How the hell did he get in there?

MUSTAFA. Just stay there, Len. I'm dealing with this. I've done it before.

SHABIR (*calm, reasonable*). Yes, you have, haven't you. And look what happened then. Is it his turn this time?

SHABIR *throws a menacing look over at* LEN. *It's enough to make* LEN *step back from the cell bars.*

MUSTAFA. That's it, Len, go, get out – I need to do this alone.

LEN. Mustafa, what's going on?!

LEN *starts to switch on the lights in the corridor. He hits an alarm button on the wall but nothing happens.*

Come on! Come on! It's not working – nothing's working!

SHABIR. Of course it's not working. It only works when I say so – (*To* MUSTAFA.) Isn't that right?

MUSTAFA. Get out, Len – now.

SHABIR. See, Mustafa, he's in it now. You should have let me keep the boy. You shouldn't mess with things you can't handle, things beyond your power.

MUSTAFA. You don't see it, do you? You're getting weaker by the day. I gave you a choice.

SHABIR (*riled*). You fucked up last time and now you've fucked it up for the old guy. Haven't you?

SHABIR looks intensely at LEN, *who grabs onto the bars of the cell door tightly. He can't breathe. The lights of the cell and corridor switch on, flicker and shine bright – too bright – we see the back wall of the cell is black with fire though there are no flames. We hear the throb of a heartbeat getting faster and faster.*

MUSTAFA. Stop!

SHABIR. Step out of there now, Mustafa, or I'll finish him!

LEN lets out a gasp, he's in tremendous pain, his life is under threat.

LEN. S... Stay... Mus...

MUSTAFA. In the name of Allah, I command you leave this place – go back – go back to where you belong!

MUSTAFA stands one hand on the taveez around his neck. He is afraid but he can see LEN's *pain.*

SHABIR. You did this to the boy and you're doing it to him!

MUSTAFA. In the name of Allah, the most gracious, the most merciful – leave this place now! Leave!

SHABIR. Who are you going to save, Mustafa – him or you?

MUSTAFA. Where I go, you go, remember? Allah Hu Akbar!

MUSTAFA steps out of the hisar and embraces SHABIR. *The lights flicker as* LEN *lets go of the bars and falls to the floor. The light bulbs burst and suddenly there is darkness and silence.*

End of scene.

Scene Seventeen

Day. MUSTAFA*'s cell. The back wall is still black, and a similar black scar marks the floor where* MUSTAFA *and the djinn embraced. The cell is empty but the door is ajar.* LEN *enters with* SHABIR. *They stand at the door to the cell.*

SHABIR (*quiet*). Thank you.

LEN. Sorry, Shabir, but I have to stay – you're not supposed to be in here.

    SHABIR *nods. He steps into the cell.*

SHABIR. I just wanted to… see…

    He looks down at the black scar on the floor. Then looks at LEN *with a question.*

LEN. That's where we found him.

    SHABIR *touches the place, sits there on the floor. He holds his head in his hands.*

SHABIR. Not a mark on him?

LEN. No. Just a trickle of blood from his nose.

SHABIR. We're waiting for the autopsy. He wouldn't have… I know my brother and he wouldn't have taken his own [life]…

LEN. No. He wouldn't.

SHABIR. Were you on duty?

LEN.…

SHABIR. What did they say? Have they said anything, what's the stuff on the wall – was there a fire?

LEN. I'm really sorry for your loss, son, but I'm not permitted to discuss the details with anyone. Prison policy. There'll be a report.

    LEN *turns to step out of the cell.*

SHABIR. I believed him.

    LEN *looks around at* SHABIR.

My little brother, I believed him. I believed him – I believed him. I…

SHABIR *breaks down.*

LEN. I'll get you some water.

SHABIR *is crying into his hands on the floor.* LEN *leaves for a moment to get some water from the cooler outside.* SHABIR *spots something in a corner on the floor, reaches out and takes it. It's* MUSTAFA*'s tasbih. As he holds the tasbih, the lights flicker, barely noticed. He pockets it and stands.* LEN *enters with a cup of water.*

There you go, son.

SHABIR. Thanks. And thanks for letting me… thanks.

LEN. Anything you need, Shabir. He was a good man, your brother.

SHABIR. I better go.

SHABIR *exits the cell and the corridor, looking back only once. As he leaves, the lights flicker.* LEN *notices this. He looks into the cell for a moment, we see from his face that he knows something happened but is not entirely sure what…*

LEN (*gentle*). Lights out at eleven, Mustafa.

LEN *switches off the lights and exits the cell. He switches off the lights in the corridor and exits the stage.*

The End.

Glossary

Asr	The third of the five daily prayers.
Djinn	Beings created by Allah from fire, as humans were created from earth. They exist in the same world as humans, but are, for the most part, unseen. Djinns are not evil by definition.
Dua	Prayer as speech/writing. One of the final parts of Salaat, in which the worshipper makes a personal prayer to Allah.
Hafiz	One who has committed the Qur'ān to heart, and is able to recite it from memory.
Hisar	Blockade. In this case, a chalk circle, used by Mustafa to create a protective barrier between the djinn and himself.
Ibaadat	Worship, devotion, dedication and commitment.
Jamaat (جماعت)	Group prayer. In Arabic: (الجمعة) al-Jum'ua. The name of the 62nd chapter of the Qur'ān, often translated as 'The Congregation'.
Jazakallah Khair	Muslim offering of thanks (Arabic). 'May Allah reward you (for the kindness you have done me).'
Kalaam	Word. Mustafa has the Word of Allah – both physically in the taveez and spiritually in the verses of the Qur'ān he is reciting – as defense against the djinn.
Mullah	Master, teacher.

Ramzaan	Common Urdu/Punjabi pronunciation of Ramadan, the Holy month of fasting in which Allah revealed the Qur'ān to Mohammad (peace be upon him).
Salaat (صلاة)	Prayer. The five obligatory daily prayers.
Tasbih	Prayer beads. A string of beads made up of either thirty-three or ninety-nine beads.
Taveez	Locket containing verses, prayers or words from the Qur'ān. Usually worn for protection.

A Nick Hern Book

Mustafa first published in Great Britain in 2012 as a paperback original by Nick Hern Books Limited, 14 Larden Road, London W3 7ST, in association with Birmingham Repertory Theatre and Kali Theatre

Mustafa copyright © 2012 Naylah Ahmed

Naylah Ahmed has asserted her moral right to be identified as the author of this work

Cover image by Indigo River
Cover design by Ned Hoste, 2H

Typeset by Nick Hern Books, London
Printed in the UK by Mimeo Ltd, Huntingdon, Cambridgeshire PE29 6XX

A CIP catalogue record for this book is available from the British Library

ISBN   978 1 84842 264 3